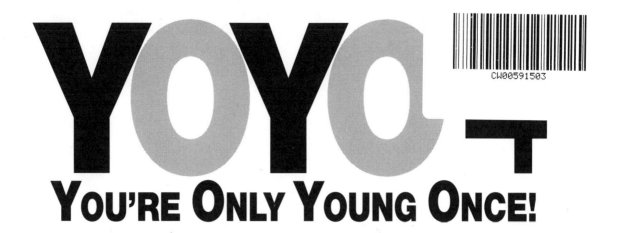

YOYO

YOU'RE ONLY YOUNG ONCE!

by

PETER GRAYSTONE

PAUL SHARPE

PIPPA TURNER

Group Bible study for over 13s

Scripture Union
130 City Road, London EC1V 2NJ

AND THERE'S MORE!

YOU'RE ONLY YOUNG ONCE! has been developed in the Education in Churches department of Scripture Union, and may be used alongside the 'Sharing and Learning Together' scheme of education and worship in churches.

© Scripture Union 1993
First published 1993

ISBN 0 86201 810 2

British Library Cataloguing in Publication Data
A catalogue record of this book is available from the British Library.

Cover design by Ross Advertising and Design Ltd. Book design by Tony Cantale Graphics.

Bible text with illustration is reproduced from the *Good News Bible* © American Bible Society, New York, 1966, 1971 and 4th edition 1976, published by The Bible Societies/Harper Collins, with permission.

Printed and bound in Great Britain by Ebenezer Baylis and Son Ltd, The Trinity Press, Worcester and London.

Books 1, 2 and 3 of YOU'RE ONLY YOUNG ONCE! are available where you bought this volume.

CONTENTS

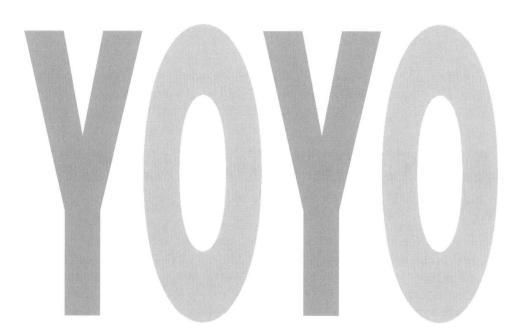

YOU'RE ONLY YOUNG ONCE!?

One of the difficulties of choosing material to use in a church setting with young people is that there are so many different kinds of group that no single scheme fits every situation. YOYO! has been devised in the hope that it will meet the needs of more groups than any other scheme. It has a thematic format and every theme is worked through in three distinct ways. Most churches will find that one of the three approaches comes fairly close to fitting their requirements as it stands. Others will find that the ideas are laid out in such a straightforward way that they can mix and match, using one of the three approaches as a basis.

APPROACH 1: *INVESTIGATOR*

This approach assumes that the teenagers taking part come from a wide range of stages of faith. Typically, some may have grown up in Christian families and progressed through the church's children's groups, others may be their friends who have little experience of Christianity in their background and attend the group for social reasons, some may have a maturing faith, while others have attended the church by habit but never personalised their commitment, and of course, some may sincerely want to argue against Christian beliefs.

There is a good deal of discussion in this approach, in which committed Christians can put their points of view alongside those whose interest in the gospel is slim. The themes are examined from many angles, but the Bible is consistently used to show that God has an opinion on whatever subject is under discussion. Although Scripture is studied in each programme, group members will not be expected to have brought a Bible with them – the passages they are asked to consider are either read to them or given in photocopied form. Prayer and praise are used in ways which allow participants to take part honestly, or to observe without feeling under pressure to involve themselves. Each programme is designed to last for sixty fast-moving minutes.

APPROACH 2: *PIONEER*

This is for use as a short epilogue or introduction to a club the main function of which is recreational. It makes no assumptions that the participants have a Christian commitment of any depth. Although the Bible is at the heart of each programme, it is not taken for granted that the teenagers will accept it as relevant to their lives – nor is it assumed that they have a particular desire to attend this part of the session. The activities are therefore attention-grabbing, and a very brief talk sometimes prompts a short discussion. This group is rarely required to pray (which would appear meaningless to non-believers). The programme lasts about ten minutes.

The third approach assumes that all its participants mean business with God and want to put themselves under the authority of the Bible as a guide for their lifestyles. It encourages them to discover how to interpret the Bible intelligently and apply its principles sensitively.

The young people will usually need access to a Bible each for in-depth study. This study, however, takes the form of creative exploration, rather than a traditional list of questions to which a 'correct' answer can be found. Basic doctrinal teaching is followed each time by discussion activities about what their practical response should be. The imaginative approaches to prayer and praise make the assumption that those taking part have a faith which they want to express. The programmes are timed at sixty minutes, but this is best regarded as a minimum so as to allow Bible studies and discussions to develop at their own pace.

MIX AND MATCH?

Because no single group of young people is likely to fall exclusively into one of the three categories, it is understood that some youth groups will find themselves mixing and matching activities from the three approaches. It is recommended that, in this case, one approach is used as a structure from which activities can be swapped, omitted or added to.

HOW TO USE
YOU'RE ONLY YOUNG ONCE!

LEADERSHIP. YOYO! is designed to be used with groups from seven or eight in number up to a very substantial size. Many of the activities take place in subgroups of four or five, with young people working by themselves. It is envisaged that one adult or older teenage leader will run the programme, with other leaders in supporting roles (taking part in sketches, distributing materials, giving a talk or instructions for an activity, encouraging the subgroups as they take part, finding opportunities to develop relationships) in a suitable ratio to the size of the group.

CHOOSING AN APPROACH. On the basis of the information given in the previous section, choose which approach best suits the teenagers you are seeking to attract to the meeting. Some churches, of course, have different groups of teenagers meeting at different times and will want to use two or three of the approaches to the same theme during any one week. If a mix-and-match approach is being used, make the selection carefully so that it includes Bible teaching, application and (except with unchurched youngsters) prayer with equal prominence.

TALKS. Bear in mind that this material is for group Bible study. It is designed to give maximum participation to the group members, and the talks have deliberately been kept short, giving only sufficient basic doctrinal teaching to ensure that the Bible study and discussions which follow have a secure foundation. Although Bible references are given so that the leaders will have confidence in the authority of what they are saying, reading them in context, not simply as proof texts, it is not necessary to read these to the group unless there is a particular reason for stressing the message of one of them. Some advice to the leaders who give these talks:

✔ Try not to exceed the time allocated, which is the appropriate length for a non-visual presentation to young people.

✔ Choose the parts of the notes that seem most punchy, and stress those.

✔ Do not read verbatim from the book; prepare your talk by writing the points you want to make on a postcard.

✔ Rehearse it well enough to be able to deliver the talk using the card only as a memory-jogger.

✔ If a brief illustration from your personal experience comes to mind, this will have a greater impact than making a more abstract point.

✔ You cannot preach an entire sermon in five minutes; be content with saying a little, but saying it memorably.

ACTIVITIES. Resist the temptation to force the group members to come to a pre-ordained conclusion during discussion activities. During activities which involve creative work, discussion or Bible study, the groups should be left to make their own decisions. The role of the leaders is to give clear, well-practised instructions, then to act as encouragers, providers of materials and time-keepers. It is appropriate for leaders to sit in on groups, since these are good occasions to develop relationships, but they should make it obvious that they are participants in the activity, not directors of it. In the same way, prayer activities should involve group-members forming their own honest responses to God as much as possible. The leaders should go home at the end of the session not necessarily having seen their mainstream Christian viewpoint demolish all alternatives, but content that a godly point of view has been put in a relevant way. The rest is the Holy Spirit's work!

CHAPTER 1

WHAT IS GOD LIKE?

WHAT'S THE BIG IDEA?

Some teenagers have little experience of a loving father in their families, and grow up seeing God the Father as a threatening, punishing figure. They need to discover the overflowing, gracious love of God, directed personally at them. Some are aware of a candy-floss, cuddly God, but have little sense of his holiness. They need to discover the awesome challenge that is set by God's absolute justice. By expanding the group's understanding, this session should heighten their awareness of God's greatness.

PRINCIPAL BIBLE PASSAGE
JEREMIAH 32:17-19

OTHER PASSAGES USED
EXODUS 3:5-6, NUMBERS 23:19, DEUTERONOMY 32:4-5, 1 CHRONICLES 29:11-13, NEHEMIAH 9:17, JOB 42:1-2, PSALM 19:1; 36:5-7; 46:10; 89:1-2; 90:1-2; 103:13; 136:1-6,26; 139:1-14, ISAIAH 44:6; 66:13; JEREMIAH 23:23-24; 32:17-19, HOSEA 11:8-9, NAHUM 1:2-3, HABAKKUK 1:13, MALACHI 3:6, JOHN 3:16, ACTS 17:30-31, ROMANS 5:8; 6:23, 1 CORINTHIANS 8:6, COLOSSIANS 1:19, 1 THESSALONIANS 5:23-24, 2 THESSALONIANS 1:5-8, 2 TIMOTHY 2:11-13, HEBREWS 4:13, JAMES 1:17, 2 PETER 3:9, 1 JOHN 1:5; 4:9-10, REVELATION 15:4

MAJOR POINTS THAT CAN BE MADE

▼ God is perfect in his love, justice, mercy, holiness, faithfulness and control.

▼ He knows everything; he is everywhere; he always has and always will exist. He is both awesome and gracious.

▼ The Bible describes God often as Father and sometimes as Mother, with every characteristic of an ideal, loving and fair parent made totally perfect.

▼ What is God like? Simply, he is like Jesus.

APPROACH 1: INVESTIGATOR

 SKETCH (5 minutes)
'Fathers and Sons'

RESOURCES
'THE FATHER HEART OF GOD', FLOYD McCLUNG, KINGSWAY

Four men in a straight line.

A: My name is Anthony Menzies. My father is Sir James Menzies, the banker.

B: My name is Martin Brown. My father is Stephen Brown, an accountant.

C: I'm Lee Alcock. I dunno who my father is.

D: I am the voice you cannot silence. My Father created the world.

A: I was conceived in my parents' holiday villa in Italy.

B: I was conceived in the house in which I now live on my parents' third wedding anniversary.

C: I was conceived in a hedge behind The Three Crowns. The pub's been knocked down now.

D: I was conceived by a miracle. My mother was a virgin.

B: I was born in Surbiton maternity hospital Greater London.

C: I was born on a number 48 bus somewhere between Balham and the terminus.

A: I was born in a hotel in the Middle East while my parents were there on a business tour.

D: I was born nearby, in the backyard of a similar hotel.

A: I don't think I like this conversation.

B: I don't think I mind.

C: I don't think.

D: I am.

A: I take after my family. I am tall, muscular

and need to shave more often than most. My mother was just like that.

B: I like to think you can see the best of my father in me.

C: I wish I knew what my father was like.

D: I came to show the world the truth of my Father.

B: My father loved me and sent me into business.

A: My father loved me and sent me to public school.

C: If my father had loved me I wouldn't have been sent to Wormwood Scrubs.

D: My Father loved mankind so much that he sent me to show them.

A: I think my father loves me, although he has never had much time to spend with me.

B: I think my father loves me, although I was scared of him when I was young.

C: Strange way my father had of loving me, abandoning me to die.

D: *(Pause)* Strange indeed!

A: I would fight for the truth.

B: I would fight for my country.

C: I'd fight anyone for a laugh!

D: I laid down my life without fighting.

A: My father said to me: 'You're going to grow up a fine representative of the family tradition.'

B: My father said to me: 'You're going to grow up to be just like ... your mother.'

C: My father never said nothing, but I know what I'd like to say to him.

D: My Father said: 'This is my Son whom I dearly love. I am well pleased with him.'

A: You can meet my father if you make an appointment.

B: I'll introduce you to my father if you like.

C: I wish someone would introduce me to my father.

D: No one comes to the Father except through me.

C: Anyone out there want to adopt me?

2 YOUR IDEAL PARENT
(15 minutes)

Explain that very often the Bible describes God as a Father (read 1 Corinthians 8:6) and, less frequently, as a Mother (Isaiah 66:13). 'Knowing your fathers and mothers as you do, you can decide for yourselves whether or not it is a good comparison!' Stress that what the Bible writers had in mind was God the greatest Father you could imagine; God the most perfect Mother you could want. So what would make an ideal parent?

Split the group into subgroups of four or five and explain that you are asking them to think themselves forward a couple of decades and imagine that they are parents with their own teenage children. They are of course going to be perfect parents without any of the 'faults' of the adults they live with currently! One by one, read out some situations they might find themselves in. After each one, allow the subgroups to discuss what they might do, then briefly report it to the others.

A It's after midnight and you are in bed. You are woken up by gravel being thrown at the window, so you go to the front door. Outside is your son or daughter plus girlfriend/boyfriend. It is pouring with rain and they are drenched. They have had their money and keys stolen. Your child's girlfriend/boyfriend lives the other side of town. Both are on the verge of tears. What will you do?

B Your teenage son or daughter has borrowed your stereo system to take to the youth club. You vaguely remember being talked into half-agreeing to this some weeks before, and decided to lend it as a good-will gesture provided it was only used for background music while the group sits and chats over coffee. However, your child set it up in the room being used for football and a ball smashed into it. It's a Cemtex job! Your son or daughter arrives home with all thirty-eight pieces. When you've had time to think about it, what will you do?

C Your teenage son or daughter wants a 'We've finished GCSEs' party. He or she has worked with great dedication and deserves a celebration with some friends. There are good reasons for letting them hold the party in your home. However, your child is pleading with you to go out for the evening so that they can enjoy not having adults breathing down their necks. If his/her bedroom is anything to go by, the chances of you returning to find the place tidy are about the same as Benidorm's chance of staging the Winter Olympics. What will you do?

D Your teenage son or daughter began making a great effort to get into college, but then three things happened. He or she joined a band to play lead guitar, dyed his or her hair blond, and fell in love. The news came through this morning that he/she has not got the right grades to get into college. Lots of tears have been shed. What would you do?

3 TALK (5 minutes)
Make these points:

God is a loving parent – without any of the faults of our fallible human parents, but with a perfect form of all the good and loving characteristics that a human parent can have.

How loving was your parent in example A? God loves humans utterly. He could not love you more; he will never love you less. He loves you totally whether or not you are a Christian. It is an endless, perfect love (Psalm 36:5-7).

How fair was your parent in example B? God is totally fair. He knows when we are being unfairly treated and will give us justice when Jesus returns. However, he also knows when we are treating him or treating others wrongly. If people sin, the fairness of his nature means he must punish them (Deuteronomy 32:4-5).

Did your parent in example C enforce rules? God's nature is to allow humans their own choices – to obey him or not to obey him. He hasn't made us puppets, but he longs that we will love him in return. He says: 'Make your own decisions, but I dearly want to be part of your life' (2 Timothy 2:12-13).

Did your parent in example D love and forgive? God has mercifully offered to bring us back into friendship with him. Because of Jesus' life, death and resurrection, God will forgive our sins and welcome us back into a relationship with him, no matter what we have done (2 Peter 3:9).

4 MY EXPERIENCE (6 minutes)
Give out photocopies of the sheet 'God and me' (page 12). Invite everyone, working by themselves, to decide which of the two options describes their experience of God at the moment. (Both or neither are allowable options.) If anyone asks, 'What do you mean by this?' say that they are allowed to interpret the alternatives in any way and may explain what they thought it meant.

5 DISCUSSION (14 minutes)
Ask everyone to return to their subgroups and compare the decisions they made, having made it clear that there are no right or wrong answers – only honest ones. If, as comparisons are made, there is a substantial difference between the decisions that members of the subgroup made, some may like to explain what they had in mind when they made their choices.

After some minutes, bring the subgroups together to continue their discussion as a larger group. Ask whether any of the pairs were hard to understand or impossible to answer. Which ones did the subgroups disagree over? Why is it that people think of God in different ways? Go on to pick out some of the pairs to help you make points about God's nature. He is both warm sunshine, in whose presence we may feel comfortable and content, and white heat, the proximity of which could burn us up in its purity. He is utterly fair in every way as a referee, but also a leader who we can follow confidently as team manager. His great love and his great justice belong together; but he is real. The fact that some do not believe in him does not stop him existing. He is God.

Conclude by giving a really simple answer to the complex question: 'What is God like?' He is like Jesus.

6 BIBLE EXPLORATION (10 minutes)
Give each subgroup eight palm-sized pieces of paper in bright colours, cut into interesting shapes (or ask the teenagers to do this). Read out a series of Bible verses, and ask the subgroups to decide on one word or short phrase (not necessarily one that appears in the passage) which sums up what the verse reveals about what Christians believe to be the character of God. They are to write their word or phrase on the shape. The verses are Psalm 46:10, Nahum 1:2–3, 2 Peter 3:9, Isaiah 44:6, Revelation 15:4, Psalm 139:13–14, Psalm 36:5, Psalm 139:7–8.

7 PRAISE (5 minutes)
Display a large sheet of card headed: 'Praise God: he is ...' and distribute some *Blu-tack*. Invite the subgroups to look through

what they have written and decide which shapes they, as a subgroup, feel able genuinely to agree they believe in as characteristics of God. Once they have sorted these out, play (or sing) a piece of solemn, worshipful music. During the music, people may come, one at a time, and attach the agreed shapes to the chart as an act of praise.

To close, read Psalm 136:1-6,26, the group responding to the leader with the repeated phrase: 'His love is eternal.'

APPROACH 2: *PIONEER*

1 *MY EXPERIENCE* (6 minutes)
Give out photocopies of the sheet 'God and me' (page 12). Invite everyone, working by themselves, to decide which of the two options describes their experience of God at the moment. (Both or neither are allowable options.) If anyone asks, 'What do you mean by this?' say that they are allowed to interpret the alternatives in any way and may explain what they thought it meant.

2 *TALK* (4 minutes)
Make these points:

❑ Christians believe that God is utterly powerful. He created the world out of nothing. He is totally awesome and in the purity of his presence we would burn up.

❑ He is also totally loving. He could not possibly love you more, for he loves you perfectly. Even if you never think of him again, he will not love you less. Even if you become a Christian this very day, he could not love you more.

❑ He is, however, completely fair and just. If people do wrong, the fairness of his nature means that they must be punished. If that were not so, evil could never be stopped.

❑ Because he is wonderfully merciful, he has provided a way for us to escape being punished for our sins. He accepted the punishment himself, coming to earth in human form as Jesus, suffering and dying before being raised to life. The way is open for us to accept his love and be restored to friendship with him.

❑ There is, however, a simple answer to the question: 'What is God like?' He is like Jesus!

(Jeremiah 32:17, Psalm 36:5-7, Romans 6:23, Colossians 1:19)

APPROACH 3: *CHALLENGER*

1 *SKETCH* (5 minutes)
Perform the sketch 'Fathers and Sons' which appears on page 7.

2 *DISCOVERING GOD* (10 minutes)
Distribute photocopies of the sheet 'God is ...' on page 13, one per person. Invite everyone to work through it by themselves, making their own decisions about their reactions to what Christians have understood to be the nature of God.

3 *DISCUSSION* (25 minutes)
Go through the eight items asking the participants to indicate where they felt obliged to circle 'No' or 'I want to believe, but ...'. (They do not need to say which of those two they settled on.) Whenever some of the group admit to difficulty in accepting a characteristic of God, spend some time discussing why it is a problem. Invite those who are readily able to accept it to explain how they have arrived at their conclusions. Try to create an atmosphere in which teenagers are able to speak their minds and share their doubts by allowing them to see the leaders do the same. In each of these cases,

bring further Bible verses into the discussion to find out whether they contribute help.

- **Loving** – Psalm 103:13, John 3:16, Romans 5:8
- **Just** – Nahum 1:2-3, Acts 17:30-31, 2 Thessalonians 1:5-8
- **Merciful** – Nehemiah 9:17, Hosea 11:8-9, 1 John 4:9-10
- **Powerful control** – Psalm 19:1; 46:10, Jeremiah 32:17
- **Holy** – Habakkuk 1:13, 1 John 1:5, Revelation 15:4
- **All-knowing** – Psalm 139:1-6, Jeremiah 23:23-24, Hebrews 4:13
- **Eternal** – Isaiah 44:6, Malachi 3:6, James 1:17
- **Faithful** – Numbers 23:19, 1 Thessalonians 5:23-24, 2 Timothy 2:11-13

4 TALK (5 minutes)
Make these points:

✔ God is supreme. He does not stop being God when people stop believing in him. There is a tendency for people to invent the cuddly, slushy, wrap-around God they wish existed, then because their invented 'God' does not measure up to what they see in our hard and painful world, say: 'He obviously does not exist.' There is no logic to that. The question is not: 'What kind of God would we like?' Instead it is: 'What sort of God do the world, the Bible and Jesus show us to be real?'

✔ The Bible describes God as a Father (1 Corinthians 8:6) and, less often, as a Mother (Isaiah 66:13). He is not the same as the fallible human parents we have on earth – sometimes great, sometimes a misery. He is the most ideal, perfect parent we can imagine.

✔ Jeremiah 32:17-19 shows us ways in which God might be compared to a perfect parent:
- He was entirely responsible for creating us (17).
- He is loving in every way (18a), as we wish all parents would be.
- He exercises discipline and will not allow people to get away with doing wrong (18b, 'parents' here refers to past generations and not just mothers and fathers).
- We must/can be in awe of him (18c), as some are of their parents.
- He makes plans for us, watches over us, rewards us (19).

✔ The love, holiness and justice of God, inseparable from each other, are vastly too much for us to understand. But there is a simple answer to: 'What is God like?' He is like Jesus (Colossians 1:19).

5 ADDRESSING GOD (10 minutes)
Give everyone a piece of writing paper and a pen. The paper should have on it the date and the words, 'Dear Father God'. Invite everyone to continue from this beginning to write a letter to God. It will be entirely private. In it they may express all they want to say to him – things they newly realise, things they find it hard to believe (even their doubts of his very existence), things they are grateful to him for, a side of his nature they want to experience more of. They may sign it using whichever of the traditional forms seems appropriate: with love from, faithfully, sincerely, and so on.

6 PRAISE (5 minutes)
Lead from this into a period of praise to which anyone may contribute by thanking God for one aspect of his nature, reading a Bible verse which has been referred to earlier, or silently telling God that they love him.

Close by reading 1 Chronicles 29:11-13 together. Tell everyone to turn to the person beside them, so that no one is left out, and say to them: '*Name*, God loves you.' Then invite them to go to anyone else in the room of whom they are fond and say the same, so that the session ends with a chorus of reassurance.

GOD AND ME

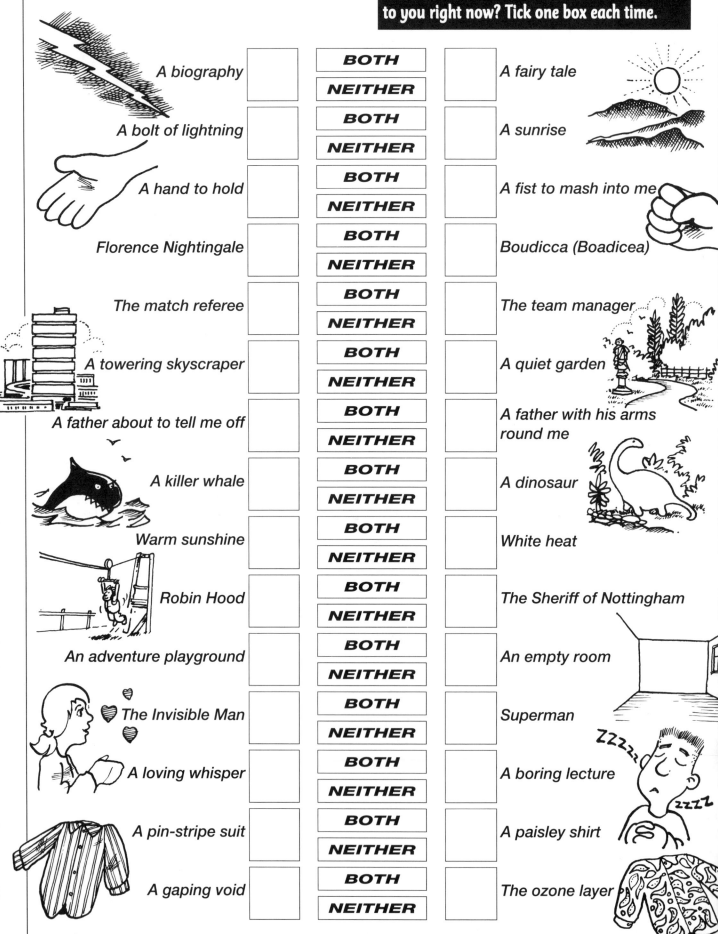

A biography		**BOTH** / **NEITHER**	A fairy tale
A bolt of lightning		**BOTH** / **NEITHER**	A sunrise
A hand to hold		**BOTH** / **NEITHER**	A fist to mash into me
Florence Nightingale		**BOTH** / **NEITHER**	Boudicca (Boadicea)
The match referee		**BOTH** / **NEITHER**	The team manager
A towering skyscraper		**BOTH** / **NEITHER**	A quiet garden
A father about to tell me off		**BOTH** / **NEITHER**	A father with his arms round me
A killer whale		**BOTH** / **NEITHER**	A dinosaur
Warm sunshine		**BOTH** / **NEITHER**	White heat
Robin Hood		**BOTH** / **NEITHER**	The Sheriff of Nottingham
An adventure playground		**BOTH** / **NEITHER**	An empty room
The Invisible Man		**BOTH** / **NEITHER**	Superman
A loving whisper		**BOTH** / **NEITHER**	A boring lecture
A pin-stripe suit		**BOTH** / **NEITHER**	A paisley shirt
A gaping void		**BOTH** / **NEITHER**	The ozone layer

GOD IS...

1 GOD IS LOVING
READ Psalm 36:5-7

God loves humans - whether they realise it or not. It is a perfect love. He could not love you more and will not love you less. You don't even have to be a Christian to be utterly loved by God.

YES	NO	I WANT TO BELIEVE, BUT ...

2 GOD IS JUST
READ Deuteronomy 32:4-5

God is totally fair. If humans suffer injustice, God will be the judge who restores what should be theirs when he sets up his perfect kingdom. If people sin against God, the total fairness of his nature means he must punish them.

YES	NO	I WANT TO BELIEVE, BUT ...

3 GOD IS MERCIFUL
READ 2 Peter 3:9

Everyone deserves God's punishment, for everyone has sinned. However, because of Jesus' life, death and resurrection, God has offered total forgiveness and reconciliation to anyone who turns to him.

YES	NO	I WANT TO BELIEVE, BUT ...

4 GOD IS IN POWERFUL CONTROL
READ Job 42:1-2

God is Lord of the universe. There is nothing too hard for him to do. He is in complete control, and whenever his power seems limited it is because he himself has chosen to limit it. He is utterly powerful.

YES	NO	I WANT TO BELIEVE, BUT ...

5 GOD IS HOLY
READ Exodus 3:5-6

God is completely set apart from the rest of his creation. He is wholly different, wholly pure, wholly perfect. In comparison, humans are as nothing.

YES	NO	I WANT TO BELIEVE, BUT ...

6 GOD IS ALL-KNOWING
READ Psalm 139:7-10

Because God is present everywhere, he knows and understands everything. There is no place I can be sent to where his love cannot reach. There is no place I can hide secrets about my true self.

YES	NO	I WANT TO BELIEVE, BUT ...

7 GOD IS ETERNAL
READ Psalm 90:1-2

God has always existed, even before he created the universe. He always will exist, and we will always exist in his company, even after this world ends. For all of eternity he has been God, and his nature has never changed.

YES	NO	I WANT TO BELIEVE, BUT ...

8 GOD IS FAITHFUL
READ Psalm 89:1-2

God has committed himself to us in a way upon which we can rely totally. Truth is at the heart of his nature. His promises are completely trustworthy and he will never fail us - even if we fail him.

YES	NO	I WANT TO BELIEVE, BUT ...

CHAPTER 2

REASONS FOR BELIEVING

WHAT'S THE BIG IDEA?

This session seeks to help teenagers understand that in a needy world, Jesus offers not escapism or false hope, but genuine and practical help. More than ever, it is good that in this session the leaders should add evidence from their own experience to the content of the chapter. Those who trust sincerely in Christ are asked to work out how they would communicate to others the reasons they have for believing in him, and are challenged to look for opportunities to witness to this.

PRINCIPAL BIBLE PASSAGE
1 TIMOTHY 1:11-17

MAJOR POINTS THAT CAN BE MADE

✔ To the weary, Jesus offers rest. To the aimless, he offers purpose. To the sinful, he gives forgiveness. To the sad and fearful, he offers peace.

✔ Historical evidence points to the truth of Jesus' claims; so does the experience of Christians down the ages, and the logic of the structure of the world.

✔ Evangelism should focus on facts about Jesus and personal experience of his worth. It should persevere despite difficulty. It should make Jesus look great, not the speaker. And it should be simple.

OTHER PASSAGES USED
MATTHEW 11:28-30, JOHN 7:37-39;
14:25-29, ACTS 14:1-20,
ROMANS 11:36 – 12:1, EPHESIANS
6:19-20, HEBREWS 1:1-3

APPROACH 1: INVESTIGATOR

1 CHANGE THE WORLD
(20 minutes)

Ask the group to form subgroups of four or five and give each subgroup a large sheet of paper on which they will make a poster. The paper is headed: 'What the world needs now is ...'. Under this caption is a large circle (drawn round a washing up bowl, perhaps). The subgroups also need some felt markers.

Invite the teenagers to talk together about the needs of the world. As they think of ideas they write them inside the circle. (They may suggest 'determination to save our resources', 'dismantling nuclear weapons', 'respect between races' and so on – the possibilities are endless.) If they run out of ideas and there is still time and space left, they should decorate their 'globe' by adding the world's features, such as Mount Everest, the North Pole, the tropical rainforest etc.

When all have finished, display the results around the wall and invite a spokesperson from each group to introduce their poster by explaining why they chose those features.

RESOURCES
'IT MAKES SENSE', STEPHEN
GAUKROGER, SCRIPTURE UNION
'HOW TO BECOME A FOLLOWER OF
JESUS CHRIST', JOHN MALLISON,
SCRIPTURE UNION
'WALKING WITH JESUS MAKES ALL THE
DIFFERENCE', SELWYN HUGHES,
SCRIPTURE UNION AUDIO CASSETTE

2 CHANGING GAME (5 minutes)
Arrange the chairs in a circle so that everyone has a seat. Ask one person to leave his (or her) chair and stand in the centre. He should

try to sit on one of the chairs. Everyone else must try to stop him/her by moving from chair to chair. When he succeeds in sitting, the person on his/her right takes his place in the centre.

As soon as the group have got the hang of the game, put two people in the centre chasing two vacant chairs. This creates a more skilful and fast-moving game.

3 BIBLE REFLECTION (25 minutes)

Comment on the way people in our world seem constantly to be chasing things that disappear as soon as they are within reach – peace of mind, fame, success, better living conditions. Draw a loose connection between this and the ever-changing game you have just played.

Give out another poster to each subgroup. It should bear a circle, similar to the first, and above it the caption: 'What makes the world...?' Ask someone in each subgroup to divide the circle into four. The first quadrant they are to head 'Weary'. In it they should write the things that wear people out or are burdensome (examples – homework or family responsibilities). The second is to be labelled, 'Thirsty'. In it they list things which make people dissatisfied with their lives (examples – boredom or search for meaning, but not literal interpretations of the word thirsty!). The third is headed 'Sinful' and the fourth 'Upset'. In these the subgroups continue to list appropriate features (for example, war in the third quadrant, broken relationships in the fourth).

After everyone has worked on this for some time, regain their attention and suggest that to the question, 'What does the world need now?' Christians would answer, 'The world needs Jesus.' What can Jesus offer to a world which is weary, thirsty, sinful and upset?

The leader should read four Bible passages, which relate to the four quadrants. After each one, the subgroups should work together to summarise in one word or a short phrase what the Bible declares that Jesus can offer in each situation. Read Matthew 11:28-30 and ask the subgroups to finish the phrase, 'To the weary, Jesus offers...' When they have decided on their response, they should write it in large letters across the appropriate quadrant (preferably in a contrasting colour). This should be repeated three times with the leader reading John 7:37-39 ('To the thirsty, Jesus offers...'), 1 Timothy 1:13-16 ('To the

sinful, Jesus offers...') and John 14:25-29 ('To the sad and fearful, Jesus offers...').

4 TALK (5 minutes)

Make these points.
There are three reasons for believing:

Firstly, it's true! The facts of Jesus' life are more comprehensively documented than anything comparable in history. The facts about Julius Caesar, which we happily accept without question, are based on much flimsier written evidence, even though he lived at a similar point in history. It is beyond reasonable doubt that Jesus lived his remarkable life and claimed to be God come down to our planet as a human (Hebrews 1:1-3). If you don't want to believe, you must call him a liar!

Secondly, it works! People who have devoted their lives to Jesus have continually spoken of their faith as a source of hope, support, purpose and joy. Jesus talked of following him as wearing a yoke, like an ox ploughing a field. However, it is not the oppressive yoke that the world puts on us, forcing us in directions we were never meant to go. It is a light and easy yoke that we can manage happily because we are not fighting God the farmer's directions (Matthew 11:29-30). If you don't want to believe you must call history's billions of Christians fools!

Thirdly, there is no choice! The Bible declares that God created all things; they only exist because he wills it and for his benefit (Romans 11:36). There is only one logical response – to offer yourself back to the person who is entirely responsible for your existence (Romans 12:1 – 'true worship' or 'spiritual worship' in most translations, but 'your logical response of worship' in the original text). If you don't want to believe, you must defy the logic of the entire universe!

5 PRAYER (5 minutes)

Ask everyone to answer these questions in a private way (either by thinking about them or writing them down):

? What weighs me down with responsibility or worry at the moment?

? What bores or frustrates or leaves me unfulfilled in my life at the moment?

? What am I doing that is plainly wrong at the moment?

? What makes me sad at the moment?

Leave a silence, during which the group may either pray for Jesus to deal with these problems or consider how they are going to approach dealing with them without Jesus' help (if that is their reasoned decision). Close with these words: 'The Lord carry the load you bear; the Lord grant you his Spirit to fulfil and refresh you; the Lord forgive you your sins; the Lord grant you his peace, this day and for evermore. Amen'.

APPROACH 2: *PIONEER*

1 STORY (3 minutes)
Tell this story:

Sasha knew that the trouble wasn't over yet. He still had half an hour of his detention to do. Today had been one ghastly event after another – and none of the trouble he was in had been his own fault.

He got his first black mark that day for being late for school. The teacher hadn't bothered to ask him why he was late, so he had not been able to explain that before he left home that morning he had already spent two hours getting the house cleaned so that his dad could go out to work and Roger was ready for the nurse to come. Roger, his brother, had Down's Syndrome, and although Mum and her boyfriend had him to stay from time to time, a lot of the responsibility fell on Sasha.

Roger loved Sasha a lot. ('About the only one who does,' thought Sasha.) And just as the nurse arrived to take over from him, Roger wanted to be affectionate. Well, you try explaining to the duty teacher that you are late for school because you were cuddling your brother! Sasha had just settled for a black mark instead.

It meant that he had to spend morning break frantically catching up on his homework. He might have got away with it if Greg hadn't started to make gay jokes about him, which really got him mad. He wasn't gay at all! In fact he was longing to find a girlfriend. He suspected that girls kept their distance because they were scared of Roger, which was ludicrous.

'Shut up!' he yelled at Greg. 'I'm trying to do the maths which you're too thick to do anyway.' Sasha didn't quite catch Greg's reply, but it had too many Fs in it to sound like an apology. The temper that had been the root of so many incidents before suddenly gripped Sasha. He grabbed his packed lunch and flung it at Greg, who at that very moment opened the door to let Mr Grainger in.

Now, it's quite astonishing how large an area a passion fruit and mango yoghurt can cover upon impact. And since two black marks in one day earns an automatic detention, Sasha had quite a long time in which to reflect on how surprised everyone was at the effortless and almost artistic way that yoghurt had dispersed. He knew full well, though, that he would be in big trouble with his dad, who would have to pay the nurse for an extra hour because Sasha was late home. And he'd probably have to pay for Mr Grainger's dry cleaning himself.

He felt sick! No one had listened when he tried to explain how unfair it was. He was worn out and furious with himself for letting his temper take control again. Who could he turn to for help? Yes! Who?

2 SOURCES OF HELP (3 minutes)
Give everyone a photocopy of the sheet 'Help?' (page 19) and a pencil. Invite them to reflect on the story, decide how much each of the people listed could help Sasha, and indicate their opinion with a cross.

3 TALK (3 minutes)
Make four points about how Jesus could help in these circumstances:

1 To those who have a heavy burden of responsibility, he offers rest. It is many people's experience that after spending time praying to Jesus, their problems seem more manageable.

2 To those who are looking for meaning and purpose in their lives, he offers fulfilment. He described it as being like 'streams of life-giving water' for those who are thirsty because their lives seem dry.

3 To those who feel guilty because they know they have done wrong, he offers forgiveness.

4 To those who are upset, he offers peace – not the sort of peace the world offers (two weeks sun-tanning in Benidorm), but the peace of knowing we are loved by someone *who will not let us down, understands us thoroughly, and knows how we feel about being treated unfairly.*

(Matthew 11:28-30, John 7:38-39, 1 Timothy 1:15-16, John 14:27-28)

APPROACH 3: CHALLENGER

1 COMMUNICATIONS (15 minutes)

For this exercise the teenagers need to be in subgroups of three, and within the subgroup they should label themselves A, B and C. (If group numbers mean that a couple of subgroups have four, they have two people labelled C.) Everyone labelled A should stand in one corner of the room, all the Cs in the opposite corner of the room, and Bs in the middle (or in a different room altogether if that is possible).

Show the As (but no one else) the diagram 'Draw this!' on page 19. Each person lettered A must then go to his or her fellow group member among the Bs and describe (without drawing or hand movements) what the diagram looks like.

Those in section B then go to their partners in section C, who have pencils and paper. They must tell the Cs what they believe the diagram looks like from the description they have heard, and those labelled C must attempt to draw it.

When all have completed this, ask them to reassemble in their subgroups of three and show them the diagram they have been trying to communicate. Invite them to display and laugh at their own and each others' efforts.

Explain that this exercise is meant to help them reflect on the difficulty of communicating to others the reasons we have for believing in Jesus. Ask them, in threes, to talk about what similarities there were between doing the exercise and telling others the good news about belief in Jesus. After a couple of minutes, invite them to share their thoughts with the whole group.

4 COMPARE (1 minute)

Invite everyone to show their 'Help?' chart to the people sitting beside them. Suggest that they compare where they put their mark on the line next to Jesus' name, and talk about their reactions to what they have heard about the help he offers. Is it worth accepting?

2 OVERCOMING OBSTACLES (15 minutes)

Read Ephesians 6:19-20, and point out that even Paul, with his enormous talent for speaking about Jesus, was aware of its special difficulties and his special need for prayer.

Again working in threes, ask the subgroups to think about all the words we use in connection with our Christian faith that would be difficult or impossible for an outsider to understand. Ask them to include theological words such as 'being born again' or 'grace', and jargon such as 'letting Jesus into your heart' or 'backsliding'. They should make a list of these down the left hand side of a sheet of paper.

Having done this, they should pass the sheet of paper to the subgroup next to them in a clockwise direction, and take the one being passed to them by the group on the other side. They should look at the words and phrases on the paper they have received, then try to think of a way of expressing the same meaning without using complicated language. For each phrase, they write their alternative on the right hand side of the page. When everyone has finished, the papers should be handed back to the subgroup that first wrote on them, who may look at them and decide whether or not the problem of conveying the meaning in understandable language has been solved.

3 PRAYER (5 minutes)

Invite the teenagers to think of one person to whom they would like to communicate the good news about Jesus. They should share the name and a few details with the others in their subgroup. Then spend time praying in threes for those people – for opportunities to talk about Jesus and for the right words to say. The leader should bring this time to a close by reading Ephesians 6:19-20 again.

4 TALK (5 minutes)

Read Acts 14:1-20 and make these points about Paul's example of how to tell others the good news:

☐ *Paul talked about four things...*
☐ *He told people the facts about Jesus (3).*
☐ *He talked about the remarkable things he had seen and done personally because of Jesus (3).*
☐ *He pointed out that some of the things humans do are worthless (15).*
☐ *He showed how the good things in creation prove God's existence (17).*

☐ *Everything he did pointed away from himself and toward Jesus (13-15). When we share the good news with our friends, they should not be left thinking, 'Aren't you great!' but 'Isn't Jesus great!'*

☐ *It was not an easy task. Paul was beaten up (19), and those who speak for Jesus today risk being physically or verbally done over.*

☐ *However, it was a simple message, and so should ours be. Karl Barth was a great theologian who thought as deeply about the complexities of faith as any other academic this century. One day his students asked him,*

'What is the most profound truth about Christianity you have preached or researched in all your years at university?' He thought for a moment and replied with the words of a song he had learnt as an infant in Sunday School: 'Jesus loves me, this I know, for the Bible tells me so.'

5 GETTING PREPARED (20 minutes)

Invite the subgroups to work together to compile a short, simple statement: 'Why I have decided to follow Jesus.' Paul wrote such a statement in 1 Timothy 1:12-17. In verse 11 he announces that this is his statement. In verses 12-14 he talks about his personal experience, and in verses 15-16 he states the facts about Jesus. Read this to the teenagers as an example of the pattern their statement might have, then set them to work.

When all have finished, invite one member of each subgroup to read what they have written to the others. Try to find something encouraging to say about each contribution. Close by challenging everyone present to be ready for God to give them opportunities to evangelise by having in mind what they would say if ever they were called on during a school lesson, or among work colleagues or friends, to give reasons for why they believe Jesus is worth devoting their lives to.

HELP?

How much do you think each of these people would be able to help Sasha in this difficult situation? Put an X on the line between the two ends to show your opinion.

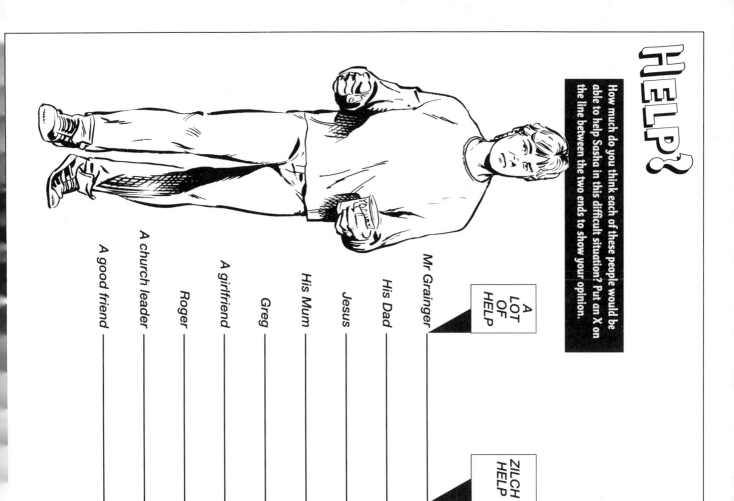

A LOT OF HELP

ZILCH HELP

Mr Grainger ——————————

His Dad ——————————

Jesus ——————————

His Mum ——————————

Greg ——————————

A girlfriend ——————————

Roger ——————————

A church leader ——————————

A good friend ——————————

DRAW THIS?

CHAPTER 3

WHAT DOES GOD EXPECT OF ME?

WHAT'S THE BIG IDEA?

This session offers an evangelistic opportunity. It invites those at all stages of faith (or none) to look at the state of their lives and make a decision about whether it is time to 'return' to God their Father. Teenagers who are committed to their faith are asked to consider how their purpose in life differs from those who do not share their beliefs and are challenged to a life of witness and servanthood.

PRINCIPAL BIBLE PASSAGE
LUKE 15:11-24

MAJOR POINTS THAT CAN BE MADE

✔ God has created us with a free choice – to obey him or to rebel against him. It is human nature to rebel.

OTHER PASSAGES USED
PSALM 130:1-4, PROVERBS 30:7-9,
MATTHEW 5:13-16; 6:19-21; 19:21, MARK
9:50, ACTS 26:9-18, ROMANS 3:23-24,
2 CORINTHIANS 5:17-18, EPHESIANS 2:10;
6:1-4, PHILIPPIANS 2:14-16; 4:8,
COLOSSIANS 3:23, 1 THESSALONIANS
3:12; 5:12-15, 1 TIMOTHY 4:8, HEBREWS
10:24-25, 1 PETER 2:9-10

✔ All must decide whether to remain in rebellion against God, or to return to him. His grace is such that he forgives and welcomes those who turn to him.

✔ Those who have returned to God live under new priorities – servanthood instead of selfishness, witness to God instead of drawing attention to oneself. We are to benefit the world God has put us in – much as salt improves everything it is in contact with and light stands out in darkness.

APPROACH 1: INVESTIGATOR

1 MY STORY (15 minutes)

Give everyone a copy of the sheet 'My story' (page 25 – make sure that the information on the following page, called 'Runaway son', is kept back at this stage). Ask everyone to fill in their date of birth and today's date. Then invite them to consider which events between those dates have been turning points for them – events which changed things either for better or for worse. They are to insert these in the boxes at the turning points of the 'road'. The leader should already have filled one in as an example to set the tone with its honesty, seriousness and restraint for the sake

RESOURCES
'HOW TO BECOME A FOLLOWER OF JESUS
CHRIST', JOHN MALLISON, SCRIPTURE
UNION
'MAKING IT WORK', STEPHEN
GAUKROGER, SCRIPTURE UNION

of privacy. Everyone may then choose some phrases which sum up their lives, adding others if they prefer.

After doing this alone for several minutes suggest that the group get into fours (find a partner, then each pair join another pair). One at a time, they may explain to each other the events they have chosen and why they feel they were changed by them. Stress that no one is to feel forced to reveal anything they do not wish to.

2 RUNAWAY SQUEEZE (7 minutes)

Play this game. Divide the group into two equal teams. Both should stand in a line, holding hands, stretching out in opposite directions from *a leader in the centre. The leader should toss a coin and, without speaking, reveal it on the back of his or her hand so that the people at the head of each team see it simultaneously. If it is tails, they do nothing. If it is heads, they squeeze the hand of the person next to them. The squeeze should get passed on until it has gone all the way down the line. The person at the end of the line should let go the moment he or she is squeezed and run back to the leader in the centre. The first of the two end players to return to the centre gains two points for the team and forms its new head. Keep going several times. If there is a false alarm and a squeeze is passed when it should not be (a frequent occurrence), the team loses one of its points.*

3 STORY (5 minutes)

Tell this story, a modernised version of Luke 15:11-24, called 'Runaway son'.

'You'll need these,' said Dad, trying to keep his emotions under control. Jake opened the plastic carrier bag. It contained a pair of boxer shorts and a pair of trainers. 'A goodbye gift,' said Dad. 'Because I love you. Because I'll always love you.'

The present was absolutely typical of Dad, thought Jake. In fact it was typical of why he was leaving. The boxers were going out of fashion and the trainers were all wrong; wrong colour, wrong laces, wrong tradename, wrong everything. A boring present to end a boring existence at home.

But he was away! He had got away! And in his suitcase a huge amount of money – in cash! 'If you want to go that much,' Dad had whispered, 'then you must go. I'll give you the part of my estate that you would have had in my will when I die. It will be yours eventually, so take it now!' And Jake had taken it! And Jake was away!

He had three ambitions: to live in a home in which his friends could party every night with no one to lay down petty rules, to own the biggest collection of CDs in Bigtown, and to lose his virginity. Not necessarily in that order.

Well, to be honest, it was a gas! He had the best buzz he'd had in his life. He achieved all three of his ambitions ... not in that order! He sank more booze than the Rover's Return. He spent more money than Barclays Bank. And he had more friends than Noddy! It was, as they say, happening!

But then it went wrong. His money ran out, which was OK until his credit ran out. Then his popularity ran out, which was OK until he discovered that the people he had been so generous to were not prepared to do anything in return. Then his health ran out, which was OK until the rumour went round that it was – well – *that* disease. Then his mates ran out. And that wasn't OK at all!

'I'll try for a job. That's cool! I can hack that!' But it wasn't as easy as Jake thought. Bigtown isn't what it was for casual labour. The youth training scheme won't look at you if you're NFA (that's 'no fixed abode'), and after queuing three hours at social security they told him to come back tomorrow. He walked all night because it was too cold to sleep.

It was eight o'clock next morning when he got the first glimmer of hope. A city farm offered him a couple of days' work. He lied about his address hoping he could hide behind one of the barns when it got dark and spend the night there. It was cruddy work – slopping out the troughs, sweeping out trash. By the end of the day he was starving, and dead on his feet from lack of sleep. His supper was the last of the rotting apples that were meant for the pigs.

As night fell, he lay down behind the sty and tried to find somewhere soft for his head. On and off he drifted into sleep. At six o'clock in the morning he heard a pattering noise drifting down the road. He put it out of his dozing mind for a few seconds, but suddenly woke up to find himself drenched by a shower of freezing water. He shot up, leapt into the safety of the pig-pen and shook himself. The street cleaner! The street-washing vehicle had drenched him! In the dreary dawn, he took off his soaking clothes and sat wearily on the wall. The sun came up on a desperately miserable man, looking no more than a desperately miserable boy, wearing nothing but a pair of boxers and a pair of trainers. And as he sat there, those rather pathetic clothes reminded him of another time, and another place, and another person who would never have let him sink to such a state.

'How do you rate my prospects, Porker?' With a sort of rumbling snort, the pig dumped its steaming reply on one of the boy's trainers. He took off both the shoes, flung them into the trough and, for the first time in many years, wept aloud.

Two days later a father, looking from the upper floor of his house, saw a sad creature at the distant end of the street, dressed in his underwear, dragging a pair of trainers along the road behind him. A son, terribly frightened, terribly alone, looked up at the moving curtains of a home he barely recognised. The father stared at the son. The son stared at the father. And for a moment, not a leaf in the street stirred to disturb the silence...

4 DIALOGUE (15 minutes)

Having reached that point in the story, stop it abruptly. Give out the sheet 'Runaway son', photocopied from page 26. Explain that this is a story which Jesus told, and that the ending is given in the extract from the Bible at the top of the page.

Invite the group to return to their fours. They are to finish the story in a way which is faithful to the original. They should write a dialogue which shows what happened when the father met the son and demonstrates what the emotions were on both sides. After they have had about ten minutes to work on this, some of them could be performed.

5 TALK (5 minutes)

Make these points:

◯ Like all Jesus' parables, this story has a point. The father represents God; the son represents human beings, you and me.

◯ The Bible teaches that humans were created to live happily and peacefully in company with God. However, he did not make us like computers, which have to do what they are programmed to do. He created us with the choice of living his way, or living in defiance of his way. Every time we do something wrong, something which would hurt or anger God, it is like the son leaving home. And God lets us go (Romans 3:23).

◯ The appeal of living a life which has no moral restraints is obvious. But it does not last. Everyone without exception reaches the point where they say: 'Why am I doing this? Is my life really happy? Are the kicks I'm getting as good as I expected them to be? What would be left if I didn't have money?' That is the point at which everyone must decide: 'Shall I go back to my Father God?' (Luke 15:18-19).

◯ Because God is merciful, he takes us back. He forgives us, restores us to friendship with him, treats us as his own children, like Jesus, and prepares an everlasting 'party' for us in our Christian life now and in heaven (Romans 3:24).

◯ If you feel far away from God, return to him now. Tell him you need him, ask him to forgive you, make plans to live like Jesus as a son or daughter of God. He will do all the rest, 'running to meet you'. Perhaps you would like to talk to one of the leaders about what it means in practice!

6 WHERE AM I? (3 minutes)

Return people's attention to the 'Runaway son' sheet. Suppose this were the story of your relationship with God, your Father. Where would you be? Leaving home? Living riotously? Miserable? Returning? Enjoying the party? Suggest that everyone draws a pin-person on the road to show where they feel themselves to be. When they have done this, ask them to put an X on the road where they feel they would most like to be (it might be at the same place; it might not). This is a private decision, not for sharing.

7 TESTIMONY (5 minutes)

Ask someone known to the group to talk about why they chose, at some point in the past, to change their lives and return to God. What difference has it made in practice? At some point in the testimony it should be mentioned that many people grow up in Christian households and are never aware of rebelling against God; that is a great privilege, and they must be sure that they know at every junction of their lives that they are still going God's way, not just by being good, but by seeking him constantly for their forgiveness and for their purpose in life.

8 PRAYERS OF DECISION (5 minutes)

Ask everyone to clench their fists lightly and to shut their eyes. You will ask them some questions and they must decide whether the answer is 'less' or 'more'. If it is 'less' they squeeze their left hand, as a sign to themselves and God; if it is 'more', they squeeze their right hand. They may not have an opinion – in which case they do neither!

■ *Would returning to God make your life more full of purpose or less?*

■ *Would returning to God make your life more full of guilt or less?*

■ *Would returning to God make your life easier or less easy?*

■ *Would returning to God make your life more exciting or less?*

■ *Would returning to God make your life more pleasing to him or less?*

The leader should say the following prayer on behalf of the group. He or she should leave short pauses in it for individuals silently to add 'yes' or 'no'. Point out that if they answer 'yes' all the time, they should consider themselves to be part of God's family of Christians and they may like to talk with a leader about what their next step could be.

> *Have I had times when I deliberately did things which hurt or angered God? ...*
> *Have I had times when my life has not truly been full of purpose? ...*
> *Do I want to live the way I was created to live, in the company of God my Father? ...*
> *Do I wish I had not sinned and want God to forgive me? ...*
> *Am I prepared to live my life his way from now on, with his help? ...*
> *Father God,*
> *out of your great love for me,*
> *everlasting love,*
> *love upon love,*
> *take me back as your child.*
> *Amen.*

APPROACH 2 : PIONEER

1 *STORY* (5 minutes)
Tell the story given on page 21, a modernised version of Luke 15:11-24, called 'Runaway son'.

2 *DISCUSSION* (2 minutes)
Stop the story abruptly and announce that you want the group to finish it. When the father and son were finally face to face, what do you think were the father's first words? Put the group into pairs and ask them to decide on a line of dialogue – it can lead to a tragic ending or a happy one; it can be funny or ironic or serious; it can be a well-known line or one they have made up – but it must make sense. Set them talking, then ask for their suggestions. Congratulate them.

3 *TALK* (3 minutes)
Make these points:

✔ The story is one that Jesus told, but in a modernised version. Read straight from the Bible the ending Jesus gave to it in Luke 15:20-24.

✔ The stories Jesus told were meant to have a meaning. The meaning of this one is simple; the father is God, the son is you. All of us have at one stage left God and decided to do what gives us pleasure, no matter how sinful or selfish or disobedient that is. Some people end up in despair because of this; some people haven't let the impact of it hit them yet – whatever the case, God longs for us to come back to him. He is prepared to forgive us for everything we have done wrong, to accept us as his sons and daughters (that means on a par with Jesus himself), and to offer us a share in his Kingdom of heaven now and for time everlasting.

✔ This is too good to waste. Think about asking God to take you back right now. If you do, simply tell him (or talk to a leader about it for more information) and you will never regret it.

(Luke 15:11-24, Psalm 130:1-4)

APPROACH 3: CHALLENGER

1 *GAME WITH A PURPOSE* (5 minutes)
Bring in some objects or gadgets the use of which is not obvious, or which are so old or rare that their purpose is obscure. You might, for instance, produce a crank handle, a gardener's implement, a part of a car, a candle snuffer, a slide rule, an egg separator, an old-fashioned kitchen implement and so on. Each

time, ask: 'What is the purpose of this object; what was it created for?' With people working in threes or fours, score this as a game.

Then produce your next 'object', which is a human, one of the group. Describe 'it' in physical terms and ask: 'What is its purpose?' Let the teenagers discuss this for a few minutes.

2 PEOPLE'S PURPOSES (10 minutes)

Pose the question: 'What are the purposes in life of most teenagers in this area?' Do this in the form of a brainstorm, in which anyone in the room is allowed to suggest an answer and a list is recorded. No one may comment on any other answer until the list is complete, and every suggestion must be taken seriously. There is a time limit of three minutes, so the thoughts must come quick and fast. Start them off with a couple of examples, such as 'to pass their exams' or 'to lose their virginity', then open it to all.

Immediately after this, hold a second brainstorm, this time the question being: 'What are the purposes in life of people who are Christians?' As an example to help them, mention the answer given by the 1647 Westminster Confession – 'to glorify God and to enjoy him for ever.'

When three minutes are up, display the two lists side by side. Ask which list sounds more appealing. If it is the first, discuss what is missing in your group's experience of Christianity which makes these other things sound more exciting. If it is the second, discuss why Christians fail to communicate to the majority of the population the appeal that the list has.

3 PRAISE AND THANKS (5 minutes)

Use this chant as an act of praise, the group responding to the leader with the words in *italics*:

You are my source of hope, Lord,
   You are my source of hope,
You are my sense of purpose, Lord,
   You are my sense of purpose,
You are my reason for living, Lord,
   You are my reason for living.
I am the clay that you mould, Lord,
   I am the clay that you mould,

I am the book that you write, Lord,
   I am the book that you write,
I am the temple you build, Lord,
   I am the temple you build.
You are the giver of life, Lord,
   You are the giver of life,
You are the giver of meaning, Lord,
   You are the giver of meaning,
You are the one that I love, Lord,
   You are the one that I love.

Follow this with an open time of praise to which anyone may contribute a sentence which declares God's greatness or thanks him for the renewed purpose he has given his people as they worship him and enjoy him forever.

4 BIBLE STUDY (30 minutes)

Remind the group of the story of Paul's conversion from a life devoted to stamping out Christianity to faith in Jesus. Toward the end of his life, he recalled – as part of his defence on trial in front of King Agrippa – his dramatic meeting with the ascended Jesus. Read Acts 26:9-18. Draw attention to verse 16, where Paul is told that his new purpose in life as a Christian is to be firstly a servant, and secondly a witness. Describe briefly what each of those words means in a Christian context.

Give everyone a copy of the sheet 'Servant and witness', photocopied from page 27. Invite the group to return to the subgroups in which they played the game, in order to study the Bible. They are to look at each category and, as an entirely personal response, note what they consider to be their present degree of commitment to it. They might, for instance, write 'Girlfriend/boyfriend – meet or telephone every day', or 'School/work/college – try to get by on bare minimum', and so on. Then, as a subgroup, they should go through the categories (they may need to be selective if it is a long process), read the Bible verse that will focus their thoughts, and talk together about what it means to be a servant and to be a witness in relation to the people and situations described. Insist that they keep their conclusions practical.

5 TALK (5 minutes)

Make these points:

● Many things in the Christian life are described in terms of darkness and light. Christians are seen as the chosen beneficiaries of a wonderful act of God which brought his people out of darkness into light. Our new purpose is to proclaim how wonderful that action was to those who are still in darkness (1 Peter 2:9-10) and to live in such a way that we stand out as different, the way stars stand out in the night sky (Philippians 2:14-16).

➡ As a Christian, you are a witness to God whether you like it or not. People cannot see Jesus in person, but they can see you and me in person, and they put a value on Jesus by what they see of us, good or bad. In that sense we are 'a light for the world', not isolating ourselves from it, but standing out in it to direct others (Matthew 5:14-16).

➡ We are also to live among people in a way which benefits them. We are to give friendship and to promote peace, not just among Christians, but among non-Christians as well. This service of good works is what God has planned as our new purpose

(Ephesians 2:10); not 'what can I get out of life?' but 'what can I give to the lives of others?' This is described as being like salt, invisibly doing its work when mixed into food. We too are, without drawing attention to ourselves, to improve the lot of those with whom we share the planet (Mark 9:50, Matthew 5:13).

6 PRAYER (5 minutes)

Back in subgroups, invite everyone to choose from the Bible study sheet one area which they would like to work on. They may, if they desire to, share with the others how they would like God to change them in order to live more as he wants them to. Pray for each other within the small group. If more time is available, go on to pray for those known to the group who do not appear to know what their purpose in life is.

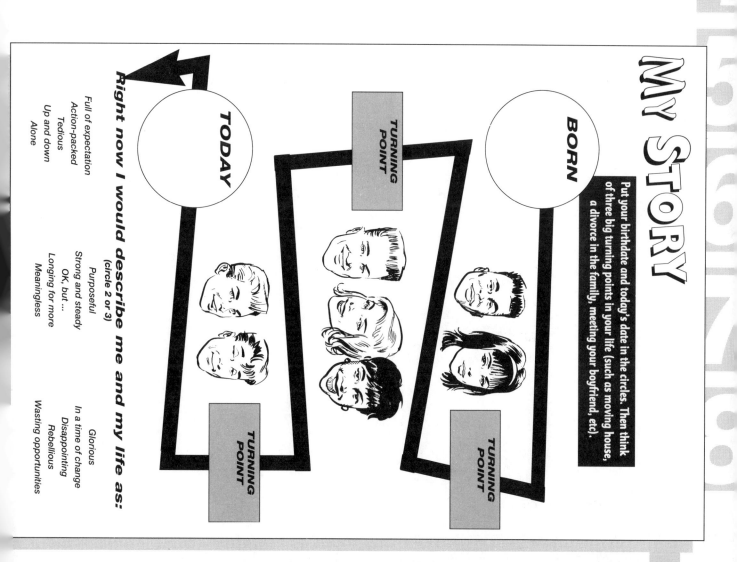

My Story

Put your birthdate and today's date in the circles. Then think of three big turning points in your life (such as moving house, a divorce in the family, meeting your boyfriend, etc).

BORN

TURNING POINT

TURNING POINT

TODAY

TURNING POINT

Right now I would describe me and my life as:
(circle 2 or 3)

Full of expectation
Action-packed
Tedious
Up and down
Alone

Purposeful
Strong and steady
OK, but …
Longing for more
Meaningless

Glorious
In a time of change
Disappointing
Rebellious
Wasting opportunities

RUNAWAY SON

There was once a man who had two sons. The younger one said to him, 'Father, give me my share of the property now.' So the man divided his property between his two sons. After a few days the younger son sold his part of the property and left home with the money. He went to a country far away, where he wasted his money in reckless living. He spent everything he had. Then a severe famine spread over that country, and he was left without a thing. So he went to work for one of the citizens of that country, who sent him out to his farm to take care of the pigs. He wished he could fill himself with the bean pods the pigs ate, but no one gave him anything to eat. At last he came to his senses and said, 'All my father's hired workers have more than they can eat, and here I am about to starve! I will get up and go to my father and say, 'Father, I have sinned against God and against you. I am no longer fit to be called your son; treat me as one of your hired workers.' So he got up and started back to his father.

He was still a long way from home when his father saw him; his heart was filled with pity, and he ran, threw his arms round his son, and kissed him. 'Father,' the son said, 'I have sinned against God and and against you. I am no longer fit to be called your son.' But the father called his servants. 'Hurry!' he said. 'Bring the best robe and put it on him. Put a ring on his finger and shoes on his feel. Then go and get the prize calf and kill it, and let us celebrate with a feast! For this son of mine was dead, but now he is alive; he was lost, but now he has been found.' And so the feasting began.

Leaves home with inheritance

Riotous life of wrongdoing

Money runs out; lifestyle turns disappointing

Miserable; decides to go home

Party to celebrate return

Father runs to welcome him back

SERVANT AND WITNESS

	Present level of commitment	What practical difference would it make to be a servant here?	What practical difference would it make to be a witness here?
Parents — Ephesians 6:1-4			
This group — Hebrews 10:24-25			
Sport — 1 Timothy 4:8			
Getting money — Proverbs 30:7-9			
Girl/boyfriend — 1 Thessalonians 3:12			
Non-Christian friends — 2 Corinthians 5:17-18			

	Present level of commitment	What practical difference would it make to be a servant here?	What practical difference would it make to be a witness here?
My favourite possessions — Matthew 6:19-21			
School/work/college — Colossians 3:23			
Getting my own way — 1 Thessalonians 5:14-15			
Church — 1 Thessalonians 5:12-13			
Local and worldwide poor — Matthew 19:21			
Entertainment/cinema/music — Philippians 4:8			

CHAPTER 4

WHERE'S MY LIFE GOING?

WHAT'S THE BIG IDEA?

The way we plan our lives from teenage into maturity dominates this programme. For those who take their progress with God seriously, it will involve a close study of the way God gives us guidance, encouraging them to use the Bible and God's direct communication intelligently. For others, it will seek to persuade them that their relationship with God ought to play a part in the way they shape their futures.

PRINCIPAL BIBLE PASSAGE
LUKE 2:39–52

MAJOR POINTS THAT CAN BE MADE

◆ The Bible is able to give us direction in all areas of life. It cannot, however, be applied thoughtlessly to the twentieth century's moral issues, because the lifestyle of the people for whom it was written was so different from ours. We must find out the *principles* behind its teaching and apply those to our decisions.

OTHER PASSAGES USED
PSALM 25:1–14; 73:23–24; 119:9–16, PROVERBS 3:5–14; 16:1–3, ISAIAH 58:9–11, ACTS 16:9–10, 1 CORINTHIANS 8:9; 9:20–21, 2 CORINTHIANS 12:20, GALATIANS 1:18, PHILIPPIANS 1:23–25; 4:8, 2 TIMOTHY 3:15

◆ The Bible is not meant to be used as a 'lucky dip' book of magic. It needs to be read intelligently so that we develop a biblical way of thinking.

◆ God is using every circumstance to shape our lives, not just our Bible reading and prayer. Other people and particular events are part of the way he gives us guidance, and so is common sense! God also communicates directly by putting messages straight into people's heads, but to be certain that we have understood these correctly, we need to weigh them against the Bible and the rest of our experiences.

APPROACH 1: INVESTIGATOR

1 THE SHAPE OF THINGS TO COME (20 minutes)

Tell the group that they are going to spend some time imagining what they might be like in fifteen years' time (say, when they are thirty). Suggest that they guess at the answers to these questions, but they are to keep it to themselves at the moment so that you can play a guessing game later on:

RESOURCES
'HOW TO BEAT THE SYSTEM', SCRIPTURE UNION VIDEO

? *Will you be married?*
? *Will you have a job, and if so what sort of job?*

? *Will you have children?*
? *What country will you be living in and what sort of home will you have?*
? *Will your current hobbies still be important to you?*
? *Will you be involved with God and church?*
? *What will be the state of the environment?*
? *Will you be rich?*
? *Will you still be in touch with your current family and friends?*
? *Will you be happy?*
? *Will you be fit and healthy?*

When they have considered all these questions, give everyone a sheet of paper and ask them to draw a pinman of themselves as they will be in fifteen years' time. Around it they draw (or write words) to suggest answers to some of the questions – as many as possible. They are to do this in secret. Drawing quality is not important – in fact, a 'hopeless' drawing is better because it makes the game more enjoyable.

When everyone has finished, pin the pictures around the room with another piece of paper beneath each. Everyone is to go round the room looking at them. They should guess who drew each and write below the picture who they think it represents.

After a few minutes, the leader goes to each picture, one by one, and asks its artist to reveal his or her identity. Comment on some of the items in the picture in a way which will build up the self-esteem of the person who drew it, and ask for an explanation of anything which is difficult to identify.

2 SKETCH (5 minutes)

The scene is the parapet of a bridge over a deep river. There are two men in their underwear balancing precariously on the edge. One holds a tabloid newspaper (**A**); the other a Bible (**B**).

A: (*Edging uneasily along the ledge, laughing nervously*) Ha ha! Evening!

B: (*Very doleful, barely listening to A all through, staring straight ahead*) Evening!

A: (*Pause*) You going to ... er ...? (*He points downwards with his finger and whistles through his teeth*)

B: Oh, er ... yes, yes I am!

A: Ah! (*Pause*) Nice evening for it!

B: Yes.

A: Should be very ... er ... (*He wiggles his fingers*)

B: Wet?

A: Yes, very wet, the river. Very, very wet!

B: (*Pause*) And quick.

A: (*Immediately*) Oh I do hope so. Do you think so? Please let it be quick. Please.

B: Yes ... drop, quick, wet, goodbye. (*Pause*) Definitely.

A: (*Doesn't know what to say*) Do you come here often?

B: No. Only once.

A: Once! Me too! Never before, never again. I mean, it's final isn't it! This is curtains! (*Louder*) This is close of play! The full-time whistle! The point of no return! The last post! The end of the long and winding road! (*Shouting*) Apocalypse now! (*He sobs*)

B: (*Dead-pan*) 'Sink into the heart of the sea ... in the depths of the waters.'

A: (*Surprised*) Pardon!

B: Ezekiel 27:27. That's what it told me to do. That's what I'm doing.

A: You're throwing yourself off a bridge because you read it in a Bible?

B: 'Sink into the heart of the sea.' There's no arguing with that.

A: It was girls with me. When she left me I was in despair. My life was empty. No one was talking to me. I was utterly alone. Not even a voice to listen to. Not a soul! I even phoned up the speaking clock for company. The clock hung up on me.

B: (*Flicks through the Bible at random and sticks his finger in a page*) John 13:27. 'Be quick about what you are doing.'

A: (*Amazed*) What! You're not serious are you? Are you really looking for guidance like that? That's ridiculous. You should be more sensible like me. I wrote to an agony aunt. (*Waves newspaper*) I told her that I felt like throwing myself off a bridge. She printed the letter too. Said if she was in my position she definitely wouldn't drown herself. (*Sobs*) She'd shoot herself to make it sooner.

B: (*Randomly reading again*) Luke 4:10. 'Throw yourself down from here. For the scripture says "God will send his angels to take care of you".'

A: You're crazy. That's no way to decide your future. Look, let's find out what my horoscope says today. (*Looks in newspaper*) Aquarius, the water man! 'A great day for sports today, especially a swim. You will meet someone who seems interesting, but he will turn out to be wet. Splash out on something new.'

B: (*Randomly reading*) Matthew 18:6. 'It would be better for that person to have a large millstone tied round his neck and be drowned.'

A: You really are in trouble. You're crazy! You need someone to look after you. Come on. I think I'd better take you home. We'll go get a nice cup of tea. Put your clothes on and come with me. (*He pulls a T-shirt on*)

B: (*Randomly reading*) Song of Songs 5:3. 'I have already undressed; why should I get dressed again?'

A: Song of Songs? I remember that name. I remember it from Sunday School. There was a verse in it. What was it now? 'Many waters ...' something! 'Many waters cannot quench ...' What was it? I remember it was a verse with stacks of hope in it! 'Many waters cannot quench ...'

B: (*Jumps. As he falls, he lets out a long, drawn-out moan, which sounds like:*) Luuuuuvvvvv!

A: Love! Yes, that's what it was. 'Many waters cannot quench love.' That's what you need to find out from the Bible. That's what ... (*He looks down*) Too late ... (*He thinks for a second, then sits down*) Oh dear! (*Pause*) Well ... what am I going to do now?

3 TALK (5 minutes)
Make these points:

✖ Christians believe that God has a good plan for their lives and that the best way to grow to maturity is to find out what he wants for them and obey it (Psalm 25:12–14).

✖ However, it is no good opening the Bible at random and hoping that God's message will jump out. If you read and learn from the Bible regularly, it becomes part of your system, and you find yourself making decisions in a way which pleases God because it is in line with the Bible's teaching (Psalm 119:9–16).

✖ If we set out to make God the most important element in our decision making, he will not let us down. He can 'speak' by drawing our attention to part of the Bible, Christians (and others) giving us advice, placing strong ideas in our minds while we are at prayer (or sometimes in the minds of others and passed on to us), even our own common sense and circumstances.

✖ If we 'stay close to God' he will honour that, not by making everything easy for us, but by giving us the most fulfilled future possible (Psalm 73:23–24).

4 SOURCES OF ADVICE (15 minutes)

Give out photocopies of the sheet 'Who advises you?' from page 34. Point out that it lists some of the decisions people find themselves needing to make. Ask the group to look at each one and decide from whom or what they would take advice on that subject. They may tick more than one column.

After a few minutes, pick out three and ask people to indicate how they voted. Go on to explain how, even though it may not be apparent, the Bible can offer a godly opinion on each of those three. It does not matter which you choose, but these three are suggested, since they illustrate different ways in which God can use the Bible to be part of the decision-making process:

A Whether to repeat a dodgy joke or gossip – the Bible gives direct and timeless advice. Don't! It's as simple as that! (2 Corinthians 12:20)

B What to watch on TV or in the cinema – the Bible does not mention 'Nightmare on Elm Street 10' by name. It can't do because it was written for a different culture which had no cinema. However, there are background principles about what we should fill our minds with (Philippians 4:8). We need to ask ourselves: what would Paul, the author of that verse, write in order to have the same impact if he were writing it today in the media age? He might have distinguished between cinema violence which glorifies the subject or incites people, and cinema violence which is intended to help us understand the truth in a 'right and honourable' way.

C Where to go on holiday – the Bible invites us to make our own choice, and then to ask God to bless our plans (Proverbs 16:1-3).

The group may press you to explain how the Bible can possibly be relevant to some of today's issues. If so, take extra time to suggest a four-part process. Here, as an example, is the most awkward issue on the list, topless sunbathing:

■ **STAGE 1** What does the Bible say about the issue? (Nothing direct! There are timeless principles that sexual intercourse should be within the context of marriage, but this is one of many issues loosely connected with our sexuality about which the Bible is silent as to what pleases God.)

■ **STAGE 2** What are the differences between the Bible's culture and ours? (It was acceptable for men in Jesus' time to do manual work in their underwear. However, such was the enforced modesty – some would say suppression – of women, that sunbathing would never have crossed their minds. Today in some parts of the world it is normal for women to go to church topless. In England that would be an outrage, but on beaches in southern Europe many men and women feel comfortable about it.)

■ **STAGE 3** Are there any timeless principles in the Bible which apply to both cultures? (Two perhaps! When living in a setting unlike your home, accept any morally neutral cultural practices so that people will be attracted to Jesus because of you – 1 Corinthians 9:20-21. If your behaviour is likely to corrupt or offend another Christian, restrain it even if you feel it is right – 1 Corinthians 8:9.)

■ **STAGE 4** If the principles were addressed to our culture, rather than the Bible's, what would the result be? (Whether you are male or female, you need to be cautious about the impact you are making on others before deciding to take up the freedom that some cultures offer. And of course, there are other arguments to consider – like the growing risk from the sun, or simply not wanting to!)

This example shows how difficult it can be to find answers in specific Bible passages when really we need to seek the principles underlying the whole Bible. That takes time. For teenagers in a hurry follow Proverbs' advice: be prudent!

5 DISCUSSION (10 minutes)
Allow the group the freedom to agree or disagree with what the leader has said. Use the following questions as a starting point for an open discussion:

1 *Does anyone have experience of God 'telling' them what they should do?*

2 *Is it reasonable to expect God to play a part in your decisions about the future, or is your own future your own business?*

3 *How easy is it to persuade yourself that a 2000 year old book has something to say about your up-to-the-minute lifestyle?*

6 PRAYER (5 minutes)
On the back of the sheet, invite the group to write down three things:

✏ A decision they have to make in the near future, even a trivial one.

✏ A long-term decision that will affect their lives in a major way over coming years.

✏ A moral decision where it is not easy to know what is right.

When they have done this, ask them to look at what they have written and decide whether they are genuinely prepared to let God take charge of their plans for each of the three. They are to look at them while the leader reads Psalm 25:4–14 as a prayer.

APPROACH 2: PIONEER

1 REFLECTION (5 minutes)
Give out photocopies of the sheet 'How do I feel ...?' from page 34. Ask the group members to draw one of the five faces in each of the circles to indicate how they feel about the present state of that area of their lives. They are to do this privately.

2 TALK (3 minutes)
Tell the group that you want them to discover some of the very few things we know about Jesus as a teenager, and read them Luke 2:40, 51–52. It tells us four things:

\# He was growing in body – so the issues in the first column of the sheet were important to him.

\# He was growing in wisdom – so the issues in the second column, or their equivalents, were important.

\# He was growing in favour with God – so the issues in the third column were important to him.

\# He was growing in favour with other people – so he was concerned about the relationships in column four.

Like Jesus, our lives should be improving in all those four areas.

3 LOOKING AHEAD (2 minutes)
Invite the group to number the columns from one to four to show which area they think is most important for them to work on in the immediate future and as life continues. Then they are to think for a moment whether God would put them in the same order if he is as concerned about us as individuals as the Bible tells us he is.

APPROACH 3: *CHALLENGER*

1 *WAYS OF GROWING* (15 minutes)

Give out photocopies of the sheet 'How do I feel...?' on page 34. Ask the group members to draw one of the five faces in each of the circles to indicate how they feel about the present state of that area of their lives. They are to do this privately.

After a few minutes suggest that the four columns represent four different areas of life – physical, mental, spiritual and social.

Split them into subgroups and ask one of each group to read Luke 2:39-52 to the others. Can they find evidence in those verses of Jesus growing up in each of those four areas? What kind of teenager does Jesus seem to be from this very small amount of information that the Bible gives us?

After several minutes, invite the group to turn the photocopied sheet over and write on the back of it. They are to decide: 'The way I would most like to develop and improve in the coming months is...' They answer the question for each of the four areas – '... physically, mentally, spiritually, socially'. This part of the programme is private between them and God.

2 *BIBLE STUDY* (15 minutes)

Read Psalm 25:1-5 and Proverbs 3:5-14. Return to the smaller subgroups to discuss these questions:

? Make a list of things that these verses tell you about God.

? To what kind of people does God give guidance about the right thing to do?

? What are the benefits suggested here of finding out God's plan and obeying it? In some ways they seem too good to be true. In what way should we expect them to be fulfilled?

Use the last five minutes of this section to bring the subgroups back into one larger group and ask them to share what they have discovered, particularly about the last question, and to query anything that is not straightforward.

3 *SOURCES OF ADVICE* (5 minutes)

Give out photocopies of the sheet 'Who advises you?' from page 34. Point out that it lists some of the decisions that Christians find themselves needing to make. Ask the group to look at each one and decide from whom or what they would take advice on that subject. They may tick more than one column.

4 *TALK* (10 minutes)

Suggest that God may use *any* of those sources of advice metioned on the 'Who advises you?' sheet in order to show us what to do (except the self-centred ones). Offer a checklist to help people who need to make decisions and want God's guidance:

A Has the Bible any general principles which relate to this subject? (2 Timothy 3:15 talks of a long-term exposure to Scripture – the Bible was never intended as a 'lucky-dip' in which answers to every question can be found.)

B Does it make sense of what God has done in my life so far? (Psalm 73:23-24 shows guidance as a long-term process.)

C How does it affect my family and friends? (Psalm 25:12-13 shows how one generation affects another.)

D What advice is being given by Christians whom I respect? (Galatians 1:18)

E Are my values in this decision godly and moral ones? (Isaiah 58:9-11)

F Are my feelings and emotions overriding what I really know to be right? (Philippians 1:23-25)

G Is there anything unusual about what is happening to me at the moment from which God might want me to learn? For example, has a talk or prophecy I have heard seemed to apply directly to me? (Acts 16:9-10)

So *any* of the sources of advice on the photocopied sheet (except, of course, the ones which are merely self-centred) might be used by God. It is important to consider not just one of the questions on the checklist, especially not the last one, which is easy to misinterpret. Instead, look for help over a range of them.

5 DECISION MAKING (10 minutes)

Give each person half a dozen file cards. They are to write on five of them any decisions they have to make, either immediately (eg, is £50 too much to spend on new trainers this week?), or long-term (eg, should I live with mum or dad after their divorce?), or morally (eg, where should I let my boyfriend touch me?). Subsequently invite them to split the cards into four groups:

1 Those for which they are totally prepared to let God have his own way.

2 Those for which they want to accept God's decision, but are not sure what it would be.

3 Those which they honestly feel unready to give to God.

4 A blank card.

There are three baskets in the centre of the room, one representing each of the first three options. As an act of commitment they are to post their file cards into the appropriate baskets. (They are to put the blank card in a different basket from the one they put the majority in, so that no one who is watching can identify whether or not they are being particularly pious.) Then the leader lifts basket one and says a prayer for strength to fulfil what emerges as right. He or she also lifts basket two, praying for clear guidance as to what to do.

6 ACTION PRAYER (5 minutes)

Display on the wall this prayer by Amy Carmichael:

> *Holy Spirit,*
> *Think through me*
> *Until my ways*
> *Are your ways.*

Each of the subgroups formed earlier should work out a set of physical actions which convey the meaning of each line of the prayer. After a couple of minutes for them to work at it, they pray it aloud, group by group, demonstrating their actions.

HOW DO I FEEL?

Draw one of the five faces in each of the circles to show how you feel about the current state of your life in each of these areas.

| Excellent! | Quite crisp! | So so! | A bit dry! | Help! |

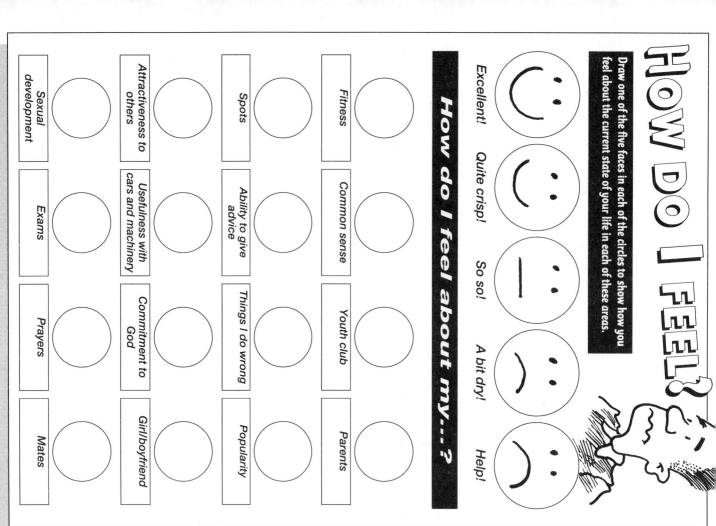

How do I feel about my...?

Fitness	○	Common sense	○	Youth club	○	Parents	○
Spots	○	Ability to give advice	○	Things I do wrong	○	Popularity	○
Attractiveness to others	○	Usefulness with cars and machinery	○	Commitment to God	○	Girl/boyfriend	○
Sexual development	○	Exams	○	Prayers	○	Mates	○

WHO ADVISES YOU?

From whom would you be likely to take advice on each of these common decisions?

	My own gut feeling	The Bible	Whatever gives me the most fun and money	Older Christians	What everyone else of my age does	My parents	Magazines	My best friend
Where to go on holiday								
When to leave school								
What clothes to buy								
Who to date								
Taking a job								
Sunbathing topless								
Masturbating								
What to buy for lunch								
Buying something expensive (like a bike)								
Who to marry								
Who to vote for								
What to watch on TV or films								
Whether to repeat a dodgy joke or gossip								

CHAPTER 5

ENDINGS AND BEGINNINGS

WHAT'S THE BIG IDEA?

This programme starts by asking why teenagers who have barely begun life need to consider death. Do we need to fear it? How does being a Christian affect the way a person considers death? It asks people who don't profess any kind of Christian commitment whether Jesus' claim to be 'the resurrection and the life' can change their view of death, while asking committed Christians to consider how the eternal dimension of their lives might change their life patterns and attitudes. It is important to be aware that this may be a highly sensitive issue for teenagers who have been bereaved or who know dying people – some of the suggested activities would not be appropriate in these circumstances. The session is designed to allow fears and feelings to be expressed without judgment, but to avoid a manipulative raising of emotions. Leaders should be available to talk at length after the meeting to anyone who needs reassurance.

PRINCIPAL BIBLE PASSAGE
JOHN 11:1-45

OTHER PASSAGES USED:
GENESIS 2:10-14, LEVITICUS 19:31, ECCLESIASTES 7:1-4, ISAIAH 25:7-8, MATTHEW 22:13; 25:31-41, LUKE 23:43, 1 CORINTHIANS 15:51-57, 2 CORINTHIANS 4:16-18; 5:4, PHILIPPIANS 1:21-23; 3:21, HEBREWS 2:14-15, REVELATION 7:9-17; 21:3-4; 22:1-3

MAJOR POINTS THAT CAN BE MADE

✔ Death faces everyone, but you can be prepared for it. Only physical bodies decay; the spiritual parts of a person are able to live forever free from pain, in peace and joy. This can transform the attitude to life of those who belong to Christ.

✔ There will be a division of the peoples of the world based on our response to God's love, and his justice. Christians know who they are and where they are going. Jesus won this victorious certainty for his followers when he was raised from death. Those who belong to him will overcome death with him.

✔ It is right and good to grieve when those we love die. Jesus did so too. However, it is possible to mourn without fear because the power of death to destroy has been defeated by Jesus.

✔ Value what will last eternally above what will cease at death.

RESOURCES
'A GRIEF OBSERVED', C S LEWIS, FABER AND FABER
'TIGHT CORNERS (A MATTER OF LIFE AND DEATH)' NIGEL FORDE, SCRIPTURE UNION AUDIO CASSETTE

APPROACH 1: INVESTIGATOR

1 QUOTATIONS (5 minutes)
Ask various people to read out these comments made by famous people about death:

66 The statistics about death are very impressive. One out of every one dies. 99
George Bernard Shaw (playwright)

66 Some day you will read in the papers: 'D L Moody is dead.' Don't you believe it! I will be more alive that day than ever before. 99
Dwight Moody (evangelist)

66 It's not that I'm afraid to die. I just don't want to be there when it happens. 99
Woody Allen (film director)

❝ I love you until death do us part and then we shall be together for ever and ever. ❞
Dylan Thomas (poet)

❝ Death is the greatest kick of all. That's why they save it till last. ❞
Glasgow graffiti

❝ I do really think that death will be marvellous ... if there wasn't death, I think I couldn't go on. ❞
Stevie Smith (poet, who later committed suicide)

❝ Since the order of the world is shaped by death, wouldn't it be better for God if we refuse to believe in him and struggle with all our might against death instead. ❞
Albert Camus (author)

❝ I hope I die before I get old. ❞
Pete Townshend (The Who, 'My Generation')

❝ This I bear witness with my latest breath, Knowing the love of God, I fear not death. ❞
Malcolm Boyle (killed in action on D-Day 1944)

❝ The Church is the only society on earth that never loses a member through death! As a Christian I believe, not just in life after death, but in life through death. ❞
David Watson (evangelist)

✖ Christians claim to know exactly who they are (precious children of God) and exactly where they are going (a totally brilliant life in God's company with no end). Because of this, they are able to get the best out of life, living it to the full because they understand both how important it is and, in eternal terms, how unimportant it is (John 11:25-26).

✖ When someone we know dies, it is good and right to be sad and to show our feelings, as Jesus did (John 11:35). Whether or not we have certainty that the person is now living in complete happiness with God, we are wise to be honest about our own loss.

✖ When Jesus was raised from death, it was like a victory over death. Those who ally themselves to him will go through the same pattern – they will die physically, but they will live forever spiritually. Christians may face death not with fear but with peace and relief (1 Corinthians 15:53-57, Isaiah 25:7-8).

✖ Jesus taught that there will be a division. Humans will be divided, not on the basis of how good or bad they are, but on the basis of whether they have received the love and forgiveness that Jesus came to earth to bring. Those who follow Jesus will follow him all the way to heaven. Those who separate themselves from Jesus on earth will not be forced to change their minds. It is an important choice to make (Matthew 25:41).

2 OBITUARIES (15 minutes)

Ask everyone to find a partner. In their pairs they may first chat about what their reaction was to the quotations. Then give out photocopies of the sheet 'Monument' (page 40). The partners are to help each other fill in the details of a gravestone for themselves. Although they fill in one each, they should compare their answers and encourage one another.

3 TALK (5 minutes)
Make these points:

✖ 100 years ago it was taboo to talk about sex but death was frequently discussed. Today the two have been reversed. However, we need to consider death because it is unavoidable. God does not want us to do this because he is morbid, but because doing so puts into perspective the things in our life which are lasting, even after death (Ecclesiastes 7:1-4).

4 CHORAL READING (5 minutes)

Present the reading on the facing page, which for the most part is based on the dialogue of J B Phillips' version of John 11:1-45. It has been arranged to minimise the number of speakers, but some of the lines could be shared among a 'crowd'.

5 BIBLE EXPLORATION (25 minutes)

Split the group into four subgroups (or a multiple of four if there are a large number). Each one is to think back over the story, seeing it through the eyes of one of four characters: Martha, Mary, Thomas or Lazarus. They should either remember the drama or be given a copy of the biblical text. Ask each group to devise the questions and answers which the character they have been allocated might go through if they

Narrator: In the town of Bethany lived Lazarus, a close friend of Jesus, and his sisters Mary and Martha. News about him reached Jesus, who was many miles away beside the River Jordan, continuing his open-air preaching mission.

Thomas: Lord, a message has arrived from Mary and Martha. It says that your friend Lazarus is very ill.

Jesus: This illness is not meant to end in death; it is going to bring glory to God – for it will show the glory of the Son of God. We will stay here for two days longer, then we will go back to Bethany.

Thomas: Master, only a few days ago, the Jews there were trying to stone you to death – are you going there again?

Jesus: Our friend Lazarus has fallen asleep, so I must go to wake him up.

Thomas: Lord, if he has only fallen asleep, he will be all right.

Jesus: You don't understand me, do you? Lazarus has died, and I am glad that I was not there – for your sake, that you may learn to believe. And now, let's go to him.

Thomas: Come on, then. If Jesus is going to risk his life, let's all go and die with him.

Narrator: When Jesus arrived, he discovered that Lazarus had already died and had been placed in a tomb.

Martha: If only you had been here, Lord, my brother would never have died. But I know that, even now, God will give you whatever you ask from him.

Jesus: Your brother will rise again.

Martha: I know that! I know he will rise again in the resurrection at the end of time.

Jesus: I myself am the resurrection and the life. The person who believes in me will live, even though he dies, and anyone who is alive and believes in me will never die at all. Can you believe that?

Martha: Yes Lord, I do believe that you are the Christ, the Son of God, the one who was to come into the world.

Jesus: Where is your sister?

Martha: I'll fetch her ... Mary, the master's here and he's asking for you.

Mary: If only you had been here, Lord, my brother would never have died.

Jesus: Where have you put him?

Mary: Come to the tomb and see.

Jesus: *(Sobs, then ...)* Take the rock away from the front of the tomb.

Martha: But Lord, he has been dead four days. By this time he will be decaying.

Jesus: Did I not tell you that if you believed, you would see the wonder of what God can do ... *(Prays)* Father, I thank you that you have heard me. I know that you always hear me, but I have said this for the sake of these people standing here so that they may believe that you have sent me ... Lazarus, come out.

Narrator: They took the tombstone away and the dead man came out, his hands and feet still bound in the graveclothes.

Jesus: Now unbind him and let him go home.

Narrator: And after this, many of the Jews who had seen what Jesus did believed in him.

---

were interviewed by Jonathan Ross or a similar chat-show host. The questions could be far-ranging, but they must not invent any incidents that are not in the Bible account and they must not say anything that is inconceivable for the characters to have said. The topics which the questions must cover are:

- *what the character experienced.*
- *what he or she learnt about Jesus.*
- *what he or she learnt about death.*

When they have completed this, each subgroup should allocate one member to play the character. A leader should take the part of the interviewer and deliver the questions which the subgroups have devised. For added impact, have a signature tune, stage set, credits and so on.

6 PRAISE AND REFLECTION
(5 minutes)

Introduce a Bible reading from Revelation 7:9-17, explaining how it captures the joy, the awe and the vastness that heaven will bring to those who follow Christ, here called 'the Lamb'. The shouts from verses 10 and 12 could be displayed so that everyone can join in the reading at that point.

After the reading, challenge the group to be aware of whether or not they will be among the enormous crowd. Be aware that those who follow him will follow him all the way to heaven. Show them this creed, based on John 11:25-27, and ask them to consider whether or not they want to join in the final line:

Leader: Jesus said: I am the resurrection,
All: *And I am the life.*
Leader: Whoever believes in me,
All: *Will live, even though he dies.*
Leader: And whoever lives and believes in me,
All: *Will never die.*
Leader: Do you believe this?
All: *Yes, Lord Jesus, we do believe.*

APPROACH 2: PIONEER

1 WHAT SCARES YOU? (6 minutes)
Lay out eight bowls, each of which contain *precisely the same number of a small, edible items – peanuts, Smarties, crisps, sultanas, Sugar Puffs, or something similar. The bowls are*

labelled: AIDS, flying, spiders, death, loneliness, violent crime, rats, darkness. Invite people to read the labels on the bowls. If they are scared of that subject, they eat two of the contents of the bowl. If it slightly scares them, they eat one. If they are not scared of it at all, they pass it by. After all have done this, compare how empty the bowls are. Announce that a national survey showed teenagers to be more scared of death than any of the others. How do their results compare? (NB Those taking part should not be told that 'death' is the subject of the session, since this would influence their voting. The bowls need to contain about twice the number of peanuts etc, as there are participants. Insist that two is the maximum people may take. This activity is more foolproof than it seems – even if participants are awkward enough to eat two of everything, the empty 'dying' bowl still makes your point about how fearful death seems.)

2 TALK (4 minutes)
Make these points:

▲ If death worries so many people, why does no one ever talk about it? Since it is one of the only two experiences that everyone in the world without exception goes through, it seems sensible, rather than morbid, to think about it.

▲ The Bible teaches that you can be prepared for death. Christians believe that when they die, only their physical bodies decay. The important parts of them, the spiritual parts that make a person unique from the rest of nature and from anyone else, live on forever.

▲ When Jesus rose from the dead, he scored a victory over death. Those who are allied to him pass through death into a life in heaven just like his – joyful, peaceful, free from pain.

▲ Christians enjoy life absolutely to the full because they know death won't stop it. It is as if their eternal life starts right now, and after death it will go on to an even more enjoyable stage.

▲ Jesus taught that there will be a division. Humans will be divided, not on the basis of how good or bad they are, but on the basis of whether they have received the love and forgiveness that Jesus came to earth to bring. Those who follow Jesus will follow him all the way to heaven. Those who separate themselves from Jesus on earth will *not* be forced to change their minds. It is an important choice to make.

(2 Corinthians 4:16-18, 1 Corinthians 15:51-57, John 11:25-26, Matthew 25:41)

APPROACH 3: *CHALLENGER*

1 DRAMA (5 minutes)
Present the reading based on John 11:1-45 (page 37).

2 BIBLE STUDY (15 minutes)
Split the group into pairs. Point out that Martha shows an outstanding insight during this incident – only the disciple Peter and demons who had been cast out had previously recognised Jesus as the Christ (the anointed Messiah, the Son of God). Ask the pairs to work through the whole of John 11 and try to identify every new thing that Martha would have learnt or rediscovered from this episode. After ten minutes, make a list of the items that the pairs have thought of, inviting each pair to contribute one in the first place, then allowing any other contributions.

3 TALK (5 minutes)
Make these points:

●◆ *Lazarus was restored to life, but like any healing which God gives today, it was just a patching up of his old body. He died again. However, Christians look forward to a completely new body after they die, and it will have the same eternal and more-than-human qualities that Jesus' resurrected body had (Philippians 3:21).*

●◆ *How can we receive this? By believing that Jesus was the Son of God (John 11:4,25,45); by submitting to Jesus' will for us (John 11:39-41); by deeply valuing eternal and spiritual things, not physical things which won't last beyond death (2 Corinthians 4:18).*

●◆ *When someone dies, Christians have divided feelings. There is grief because of the* loss, and that is OK (John 11:35). But there need not be fear, because Jesus has taken away death's power to destroy (Hebrews 2:14-15).

●✝ Being alive and working out God's purpose is very important, so don't feel bad about not wanting to die. But our guaranteed and vastly better eternal life is much more important. It has already begun the day we began to let Jesus take control, and we can thrill to the fact that nothing can halt it (Philippians 1:21-23).

4 DISCUSSION (15 minutes)

Initiate a discussion about this subject. The following questions could be used to encourage contributions:

A Read 2 Corinthians 5:4. Paul writes several times of longing to die. That was all very well in a church which was persecuted and suffering, but should we feel like that now? Does it matter if we feel so much of a longing to live that death seems a bad prospect?

B The Bible is absolutely clear that we should not attempt to communicate with those who have died (Leviticus 19:31). Why is that good advice?

C What practical difference should people notice between the lifestyles of Christians who know that their spiritual life will go on forever, and others who believe that death finishes everything or just hope for the best?

5 IS IT IN THE BIBLE? (15 minutes)

Give out copies of the sheet 'We asked ...' from page 41. Explain that picture language features in nearly all the references to heaven and hell in the Bible, and this has strongly influenced the way we visualise them:

■ 'Paradise' is a Persian word. It means an exquisite garden, particularly one that a king or queen might have. It suggests tranquillity, colour, perfume, a place of renewal, and the presence of a truly great person. The garden of Eden is called Paradise, and the garden city in Revelation is called Paradise too. (Genesis 2:10-14, Luke 23:43, Revelation 22:1-3)

■ 'Gehenna' was the word Jesus used for hell. This was a valley beside Jerusalem. It was the local rubbish tip – the bodies of executed criminals were thrown there (Jesus would have been buried there had not Joseph of Arimathea intervened). Maggots and worms infested the rubbish and bonfires were kept ablaze night and day to destroy the refuse and keep the risk of infection down. (Matthew 22:13; 25:41)

Most Christians believe that they are not expecting a garden with real grass and that hell will not be a bonfire with real flames. However, it is clear that there will be a definite division. Those who follow Christ will live with him in endless joy. Those who reject him will be faced with the unending sorrow of being separated from him (some think they will cease to exist in any form at all). There is a choice to be made. (Revelation 21:3-4, Matthew 25:31-33)

After this, ask the pairs to read through the comments of the teenagers and discuss how close they came to a genuine understanding of heaven. Is this the way most people think about life after death in the experience of the group? How would they themselves have answered the question?

6 PRAYER (5 minutes)

Ask the pairs to share with each other concerns they have for particular friends who have not yet found faith in Jesus. They might mention them by name, then pray in their pairs, aloud or silently, that they will have wisdom when speaking to these people, and that they may eventually share heaven with them.

Close by using these words of dedication, spoken together:

Lord God, here are our lives,
Here they are, offered to you,
Given in sadness, given in gladness;
Given for the joy of living, given for the security of dying;
Given for determined service on earth, given for everlasting rest in heaven;
Given because you have loved us from the beginning,
Given because you will love us until the end;
You have the words of eternal life, and we will never die.
Lord God, here are our lives,
Here they are for now; here they are for ever.

MONUMENT

· NAME ·

· DATE OF BIRTH ·

· DATE OF DEATH ·

· CAUSE OF DEATH ·

· GREATEST ACHIEVEMENT ·

· UNFULFILLED AMBITION ·

· FEELINGS ABOUT FUTURE AFTER DEATH ·

· BEST THING PEOPLE SAID AT FUNERAL ·

· LAST WORDS ·

MONUMENT

WE ASKED

... a group of teenagers outside a school in London what they thought heaven would be like.

I WOULDN'T WANT TO GO THERE. I'D SOONER BE HERE. I'D MISS THE TV.

NO POLLUTION, NO NOISE. JUST PEACEFUL. THERE WILL BE THE SOULS OF ALL OF US. BUT YOU WON'T RECOGNISE THEM BECAUSE YOU SEE RIGHT THROUGH THEM.

IT WILL BE FULL OF TREES LIKE THE GARDEN OF EDEN. PEOPLE WILL LOOK LIKE HUMANS BUT THEY WON'T AGE THERE – EVERYONE WILL LOOK FORTY. I DON'T THINK I'M READY TO GO THERE, BUT I KNOW YOU HAVE TO BE READY OR YOU WON'T GET IN. IT'S SCARY!

I DON'T BELIEVE IN IT. I BELIEVE THERE WILL BE SOME SORT OF LIFE AFTER DEATH BUT NOT IN HEAVEN. IT'S WEIRD YOU ASKING 'CAUSE I'M GOING OUT WITH A VICAR'S DAUGHTER.

ANGELS WITH WINGS AND A HALO. YELLOW AND WHITE EVERYWHERE. A GATE ACROSS THE FRONT

THERE WILL BE MUSIC BUT IT WILL ALL BE CLASSICAL. IT'LL BE BORING. WE'D BETTER PACK SOME TAPES BEFORE WE GO.

THERE WILL BE TREES. ALL NICE – NOT LIKE THIS COUNTRY. THERE WILL BE LOADS OF CHILDREN HAPPY. NOT CLOUDS OR ANGELS – I CAN'T RELATE TO THAT. NO PAIN – YOU'LL ENJOY YOURSELF MORE. I'M LOOKING FORWARD TO IT. YOU WILL SEE GOD.

... and here are some of the things that the Bible says – all in picture language.

Wolves and sheep will live together in peace, and leopards will lie down with young goats. Calves and lion cubs will feed together, and their calves and cubs will lie down in peace. Lions will eat straw as cattle do, Even a baby will not be harmed if it plays near a poisonous snake. On Zion, God's sacred hill, there will be nothing harmful or evil.

Isaiah 11:6–9

Then there came from the throne the sound of a voice, saying, 'Praise our God, all his servants and all people, both great and small, who have reverence for him!' Then I heard what sounded like a large crowd, like the sound of a roaring waterfall, like loud peals of thunder. I heard them say, 'Praise God! For the Lord, our Almighty God, is king! Let us rejoice and be glad; let us praise his greatness! For the time has come for the wedding of the Lamb, and his bride has prepared herself for it ... Happy are those who have been invited to the wedding feast of the Lamb.

Revelation 15:5–9

As for this useless servant – throw him outside in the darkness; there he will cry and grind his teeth... Then he will say to those on his left, 'Away from me, you that are under God's curse! Away to the eternal fire which has been prepared for the Devil and his angels! ... These, then will be sent off to eternal punishment, but the righteous will go to eternal life.

Matthew 25:30, 41–46

The poor man died and was carried by the angels to sit beside Abraham at the feast in heaven. The rich man died and was buried, and in Hades, where he was in great pain, he looked up and saw Abraham, far away, with Lazarus at his side. So he called out, 'Father Abraham! Take pity on me, and send Lazarus to dip his finger in some water and cool my tongue, because I am in great pain in this fire!'

Luke 16:22–24

PRAYER

WHAT'S THE BIG IDEA?

Many teenagers see prayer as a duty to undertake, so this chapter presents it as an opportunity to take advantage of. To fail to pray is not a sin, but a waste! The session deals with the problems which lodge in many minds – why does God sometimes appear to be silent and, when I do not get what I ask for, has something gone wrong? All three approaches (even approach two) provide more developed opportunities than usual to pray effectively.

PRINCIPAL BIBLE PASSAGE
PSALM 86:6–17

MAJOR POINTS THAT CAN BE MADE

♦ God responds to our prayer in the way that is best, not the way that seems best to us. Sometimes these are not the same thing.

♦ The Holy Spirit's function is to perfect our clumsy prayer, strengthen our weak prayers, and translate our poorly expressed prayers.

♦ Every kind of prayer is acceptable to God, no matter where or how we pray.

♦ God longs for honesty, simplicity, enjoyment, regularity, thankfulness, and willingness to listen to him.

OTHER PASSAGES USED
PSALM 69:1-3, 13-15,29-33, JEREMIAH 42:2-6, MATTHEW 6:5-13; 7:9-11; 18:20, MARK 10:35-45; 14:32-44, LUKE 18:1-8, JOHN 16:23-24, ACTS 2:42, ROMANS 8:26-27, 2 CORINTHIANS 12:7-10, EPHESIANS 3:17-21, 1 THESSALONIANS 5:16-20, 1 TIMOTHY 2:1-3, JAMES 5:13-16

APPROACH 1: INVESTIGATOR

1 QUESTIONNAIRE (10 minutes)
Around the walls, display large sheets of paper bearing the statements below and four sections in which everyone may put ticks to indicate which answer is closest to their experience.

RESOURCES
'PRAYER PACESETTING', JOHN EARWICKER, SCRIPTURE UNION

A I pray to God...
- ☐ Very occasionally
- ☐ Once a week
- ☐ Daily
- ☐ Frequently during the day

B This makes me pray to God...
- ☐ Crisis
- ☐ Habit
- ☐ Thankfulness
- ☐ Need

C God seems light years away and silent...
- ☐ Always
- ☐ Often
- ☐ Sometimes
- ☐ Never

D God responds to my prayers...
- ☐ Always
- ☐ Often
- ☐ Sometimes
- ☐ Never

E My prayers are getting...
- ☐ Answered
- ☐ Stronger
- ☐ Rarer
- ☐ Non-existent

F Prayer benefits...

☐ God
☐ Me
☐ Others I pray for
☐ The world

G I find praying on my own...

☐ The best way
☐ Easy
☐ Difficult
☐ Not worth the effort

H I find praying in a group...

☐ The best way
☐ Easy
☐ Difficult
☐ Not worth the effort

When all have voted, total the scores and comment on the group's collective feelings about prayer.

2 *TALK* (5 minutes)
Make these points:

☐ *God gave us prayer for our benefit, not for his. If we ignore prayer, we waste the chance to be in communication with the most powerful force conceivable. Failing to pray does not diminish God's power, it just prevents it being freed to work in us (John 16:23-24).*

☐ *But God doesn't always give me what I ask for! God will give us what best fits his perfect plan, which is not the same thing. He will not give us anything that will harm us or be second best, even if we ask for it (Matthew 7:9-11).*

☐ *But I don't know what to say! The job of the Holy Spirit is to take our prayers into God's presence, corrected, made perfect and changed into a form that complies with God's plan. We can make as much of a mess of praying as is possible to imagine; it doesn't matter, because the Holy Spirit is getting our prayers right for us (Romans 8:26-27).*

☐ *But praying is hard! There is no one way that God demands we pray. He hears when we are alone in a room (Matthew 6:6), when we are in twos and threes (Matthew 18:20), or when a whole church is together (Acts 2:42). Find a way you are comfortable with, or just shout to God for help when there is an emergency – he will respond, whether his answer is yes or no. Failing to pray is not a sin – it's just a waste!*

3 REASONS FOR PRAYING 1
(10 minutes)

Read 1 Timothy 2:1-3 to the group. The first good reason for praying is that it pleases God. He wants us to pray because that is his way of keeping in contact with his people. He asks us to express how great and loving he is, to acknowledge that we have done wrong and need forgiveness, to thank him for the good things we have – all these not because he needs any of them, but because he is pleased by them.

Split the group into subgroups of three or four. Give each subgroup a sheet of coloured card, a felt marker, and the text of Psalm 86:6-17, photocopied from page 48. Invite them to read this through – a prayer written as a song lyric. They should, as a joint decision, select one phrase from it which they could address to God as an honest statement from the subgroup. It could be a message of praise, such as: 'How great is your constant love.' It could be a phrase which admits to a sinner's need of God: 'Turn to me and have mercy on me'..Or it could be a statement of genuine uncertainty about God: 'Show me proof of your goodness.' The selected phrase should be written in large letters in the centre of the sheet of card. If there is time left, it could be decorated.

4 REASONS FOR PRAYING 2
(10 minutes)

The second reason for praying is that it is for our own benefit. Read James 5:13-14. God did not give us prayer as an extra burdensome rule for us to obey. He gave it because he wants us to ask for what is good for us. James wants us to pray not just when there is an emergency, but also when things are going well. Those who pray really have all to gain and nothing to lose.

Give out filecards, pencils and paste to the subgroups. Ask them to talk together about things they need, things they hope for, things they enjoy, and so on. They may talk about anything that they think would benefit from God's help or support, and it can include concerns of their family, the church group and their immediate circle too. Advise them not to mention anything particularly private. As each new idea emerges, they are to write it legibly on a filecard. It should be written bluntly, with no 'Amen', 'Dear God' or other religious language. An example might be: 'Help me pass my driving test' or 'Please make Siobhan's mum better'. These are to be pasted on the sheet of card around the edges of the phrase the group wrote (leaving a margin on all sides).

5 REASONS FOR PRAYING 3 (15 minutes)

Christians should also pray for the world they live in. In Israel, six centuries before Jesus, the people found themselves at war and sensed that defeat was imminent. The army leaders asked Jeremiah to pray for them. Read Jeremiah 42:2-6. Important in Jeremiah's prayer was not just his appeal to God for the people, but his use of prayer to allow God to address him as well. It is frequently during prayer that God puts thoughts into our heads which show us what we should do in response to the things we are talking to him about. In fact, in the case of the army officers, they deliberately did not do what God required of them (verse 6) and all did *not* go well with them.

Give each subgroup a recent newspaper and some scissors. Ask them to go through it, cutting out headlines and photographs which represent major concerns in the world which they want God to put right. As they do so, they should talk about what God might want them to do in personal response to these situations. The cuttings should be pasted around the edges of the sheets.

6 REFLECTION (5 minutes)

The complete sheets should be posted on the walls. Everyone is then given several minutes to walk around and look at each others' contributions. Ask for this to be done in silence so that those who wish to may personalise the prayers of others by quietly telling God that they agree. Explain to them that 'Amen' means 'so be it', or 'I am in agreement'. To say 'Amen' silently as they read each prayer would indicate to God that they wish to ally themselves with it.

7 PRAYER (5 minutes)

Invite subgroups to join together so that slightly larger groups of six or seven are formed. They should put their arms round each others' shoulders and bow their heads, rugby scrum style. In this position, the leader should call out items for which the group could all pray, extending the ideas given on the posters. If experience has shown the group to be largely agnostic, suggest that each time he or she says 'Amen', the subgroups chant:

> **God, if you're there,
> Answer our prayer.**

With a group that is more used to accepting the validity of prayer, use the chant:

> **God, you are mighty,
> Answer our prayer.**

To close, the leader reads Ephesians 3:17-21 as a prayer for the group.

APPROACH 2: PIONEER

1 SKETCH (3 minutes)

A headmaster in a gown addresses assembly from a lectern.

HEADMASTER: School, will you please stand for prayer. Almighty God, who seest our every move and hearest our every thought, and even now seest Sharon Wilkins whispering in the back row and longest for her to pay attention now, and I mean now, thou art to be praised because of thine exceeding (Arden do your trousers up and see me after assembly) holiness and greatness.

Make us thy respectful and obedient children, always ready to obey the rules that thou hast set through the ministrations of those who have given their lives to serve us despite pathetically poor pay and conditions which fall far short of comparable employment in the rest of Europe. Particularly we ask thee to show those who have been smoking in the toilets the error of their ways and make them put their cigarettes in the bin outside my office at 11am so that there need not be a detention on Friday afternoon.

And God of compassion, whose mercy and forgiveness are new every morning, grant that the message will penetrate the thick skulls of form 4D that if I catch them once more drawing in such a lewd manner on Mrs Drooper's *blackboard there will be hell to pay and their punishment will know no end.*

We commit to thee the endeavours of the football B-team in their last match of the season. Thou teachest us that it is not the winning that counts but the way we play, so we ask thee to convict our sweeper, Hacker Shinwell, of that if the opposition gets near the penalty area or I shall want words with him. May the team play above their station, Lord God; turn our B-team into A-men. Amen.

anything that will harm us or be second best, even if we ask for it.

✔ What should I say? Forget the fancy phrases that you may hear. Don't even worry about saying 'Amen' (which only means 'I agree') or kneeling. Just sit down and tell God what you mean, as if he was next to you. Try it out! It isn't a sin not to pray, but it is a waste!

(James 5:13-16, Matthew 7:9-11, Psalm 86:6-7)

2 TALK (3 minutes)
Make these points:

✔ Most people's experience of prayer doesn't go much beyond the one in the sketch. No wonder they don't bother to pray. Christians believe in prayer not as a burdensome rule to stop God getting angry, but as communication with God about specific things which can change the world.

✔ What should I pray for? Anything! People in trouble should ask God to help. People who are happy should thank God for it. People who need things should ask God for them. People who know they have done wrong can lose the guilt of it by asking God to forgive them. It is there for our benefit – and God's, because it pleases him!

✔ Why doesn't God give me what I ask for? God will give us what best fits his perfect plan – sometimes that is what we ask for and sometimes not. He will not give us

3 TRY IT! (4 minutes)
Suggest that they try it! Give everyone present a filecard, on which is written:

> **God, I need ...**
> **God, the world needs ...**
> **God, I'm sorry that ...**
> **God, thanks that ...**

Explain that they may complete any of these phrases, if they are honest about it. They may write it down, but need not if they do not want to. The leader should offer to go on praying for the things they have told God about if they give him the card. Assure them that you believe God has seen what they have written or thought, and will answer in the way which will ultimately be best for them.

Ask them to stay silent while you say this prayer, from Psalm 86:15-17, on their behalf. 'You, O Lord, are a merciful and loving God, always patient, always kind and faithful. Turn to me and have mercy on me ... Show me proof of your goodness, Lord. Amen.'

APPROACH 3: CHALLENGER

1 PROBLEMS (10 minutes)
Give everyone a copy of the questionnaire 'Me and my prayers', presented on page 48. They are to mark an X on the line somewhere between one extreme and the other to represent where their own experience fits between the two answers given. After several minutes, invite everyone to turn to their neighbour and compare their results. Are there any points about which they have disagreed markedly? If so, they may explain to their partners the thinking behind their decisions.

2 TALK (5 minutes)
Make these points:

God is longing to answer our prayers (Luke 18:1-8). Some of Jesus' parables tell us what God is like. A few, of which the story of the unjust judge is one, show us what God is absolutely not like. If even that corrupt judge gives the widow what she needs, just think how much more our perfect God will respond to our prayers of need.

Jesus taught his disciples how to pray (Matthew 6:9-13). Note that the Lord's Prayer

is a pattern for prayer, not just a form of words to be repeated. This is the pattern: praise God (9), pray for God's action in the world (10), pray for personal needs (11), repent and ask for forgiveness (12), pray for protection (13).

*The Bible gives no rules as to when or how often we should pray. It presents prayer as something given for our benefit, as well as to please God. It asks for honesty rather than showing off (Matthew 6:5), simplicity rather than 'religious jargon' (Matthew 6:7), joyfulness rather than 'Oh no, I've got to pray again' (1 Thessalonians 5:16), regularity rather than crisis binges (1 Thessalonians 5:17), thankfulness as well as requests (1 Thessalonians 5:18), awareness that the Holy Spirit may be bringing God's message to us as well as ours to him (1 Thessalonians 5:19-20).*

*Don't be afraid to pray. It's too good a provision to ignore. Don't worry about getting it wrong. Even if we make a complete hash of it, the Holy Spirit will get our prayers right for us when they reach God's presence. That's what he does (Romans 8:26-27).*

3 BIBLE STUDY (20 minutes)

Remind the gathering that the most common stumbling block that people have with prayer is that God sometimes seems not to answer us, staying silent or withholding things which would seem to be the best solutions we could imagine. Why? We can only respond with trust that God knows best and that what we asked for would have been second-best for us in his eternal, world-wide plan. To see this in practice, look at several occasions in the Bible when requests to God were not granted – is there any reason?

Split the teenagers into subgroups and give them each one of these passages: Mark 10:35-45, 2 Corinthians 12:7-10, Mark 14:32-44, Psalm 69:1-3,13-15,29-33. (Obviously, the same passage could be given to more than one subgroup, or two passages to one group, if numbers dictate that.) In each case they are to read it and answer these questions:

A What is asked of God or Jesus here?

B What happens instead of the hoped-for result?

C What learning takes place about the nature of the Christian life from this negative answer?

D What general conclusion *might* we be able to draw?

When everyone has had several minutes to work at this, ask one spokesman from each group to tell the others what their passage was about and what conclusion they have drawn. The leader should try to pull together the strands and sum up the discoveries.

4 WAYS OF PRAYING (10 minutes)

With the whole group together, ask everyone to brainstorm all the different ways of praying that they can think of. They should call out their ideas one at a time, without making comments (either negative or positive) about each others' ideas until the end of the exercise. The list will probably include: alone, in a group, as a congregation, praise, repentance, intercession, responsive prayers, meditation, on a walk, in silence, in tongues privately, in tongues publicly with interpretation, saying thank you, prayers which are drawn, prayers which are written, kneeling, sitting, standing, lying down, huddled in a circle. Suggest these only if the group are unclear as to what sort of ideas are expected.

As these are suggested, the leader writes each on a separate file card, which he tosses onto the floor in the centre of the group. Working together, the group then sorts them into three piles – those they are all happy to take part in, those they all find unhelpful, and those which belong in neither pile. Go through this pile one at a time, allowing those who find a particular method valuable to explain what they get out of it.

5 PRAYERS (15 minutes)

Use several methods of praying. Try to use at least one which would stretch the group's experience beyond what they are used to. Some options are:

1 Use Psalm 86 as a prayer. Read it antiphonally, from photocopies of the sheet on page 48.

2 Split into fours. Strictly controlled by the leader, give each of the four in turn thirty seconds to say what the best and worst things were about their past week. Then go round again, with thirty seconds to say what the most significant things will be in the next week. Then, one by one, everyone prays for the person on his or her left in the foursome.

3 Ask everyone to write on a piece of paper a conclusion to the phrase, 'Because God deeply loves me ...' The leader should collect them, order them, and read them out as a psalm.

4 Everyone in silence, with eyes shut, imagines Jesus sitting on a chair the other side of the room. The leader explains: 'He is assuring you he loves you, he wants the very best for you, you are special to him, you need not be afraid. In the silence, receive Jesus' love, ask him to tell you what he wants to say to you, and to show you what he wants you to do for him. Every time something distracts you, or a worry about yourself comes into your head, imagine yourself getting up, carrying the worry to Jesus, leaving it in his lap, and going back to your seat without it.' Continue in silence for three or four minutes.

5 Invite everyone to call out, 'Thank you, God, for ...', one after the other, adding only one word or a short phrase in this quick-fire volley of thanks.

6 If you are meeting in a church building, go for a walk from room to room, stopping in each to pray for the particular activities that take place in it. For example, pray for the church's children in the room where the creche is accommodated, in the kitchen pray for the church's social events, in the room where musicians practise pray for the church's worship, and so on. End up in the street outside the church and pray for the neighbourhood it serves.

7 Use this prayer to glorify Jesus, the group responding to the leader with the words *in italics:*

> As the sun in all its brightness,
> *Such is Jesus Christ in glory,*
> As the snow in all its whiteness,
> *Such is Jesus Christ in glory,*

> As the lightning, as the thunder,
> *Such is Jesus Christ in glory,*
> As the sky at night in wonder,
> *Such is Jesus Christ in glory,*
> As the ocean in its deepness,
> *Such is Jesus Christ in glory,*
> As the mountain in its steepness,
> *Such is Jesus Christ in glory,*
> As the hurricane in power,
> *Such is Jesus Christ in glory,*
> As the beauty of the flower,
> *Such is Jesus Christ in glory,*
> As the rich, life-giving blood,
> *Such is Jesus Christ in glory,*
> Utterly, supremely God,
> *Such is Jesus Christ in glory.*

8 Give out recent newspapers and ask everyone to choose one headline or, preferably, one picture. They, in turn, show their picture to the rest of the group and, as everyone looks at it, explain why they chose it as a subject which they want to bring to God in prayer. Having explained it, they say: 'Lord, in your mercy. ...' Everyone replies: 'Hear our prayer.'

9 Stand in a circle, arms around each others' shoulders, rugby scrum style, or lie on the floor with feet together like the spokes of a wheel and holding hands. In this position, pray for the group and particular needs of members in it.

10 Invite the Holy Spirit to come down and lead your worship spontaneously, prompting those present to suggest a particular song is sung, read a verse from the Bible, say prayers and words of praise in English, or in tongues with others interpreting.

11 Close with this traditional blessing of the Iona Community, spoken together:

> *Deep peace of the running wave to you,*
> *Deep peace of the flowing air to you,*
> *Deep peace of the quiet earth to you,*
> *Deep peace of the shining stars to you,*
> *Deep peace of the Son of peace to you.*
> *Amen.*

ME AND MY PRAYERS

Put a cross on the line somewhere between the two extremes to show which answer is nearer your own experience.

I pray because God would be angry if I didn't.	I pray because life has proved to be better that way.
I pray expecting God to respond.	I pray in the vague hope that it will help.
I am most at ease praying alone.	I am most at ease praying in a group.
I pray about many little things.	I pray when a crisis prompts it.
My prayers are getting more faithful.	My prayers are practically dead.
When I pray, God is silent.	When I pray, God responds.
Prayer is my list of requests to God.	Prayer is God's uninterrupted message to me.
I pray using my normal language.	I pray with a special voice and religious words.
When I don't feel like praying, I don't.	When I don't feel like praying, I persevere.
When God says no he has let me down.	When God says no I accept that he knows best.
When answers to prayer are not obvious, God has responded.	When answers to prayer are not obvious, God has not heard.
When God says yes I say thank you.	When God says yes I'm astonished at my good luck.

A PSALM
Psalm 86:6-17

Listen, Lord, to my prayer;
    hear my cries for help.
I call to you in times of trouble,
    because you answer my prayers.

There is no god like you, O Lord,
    not one has done what you have done.
All the nations that you have created
    will come and bow down to you;
    they will praise your greatness.
You are mighty and do wonderful things;
    you alone are God.

Teach me, Lord, what you want me to do,
    and I will obey you faithfully;
    teach me to serve you with complete
    devotion.
I will praise you with all my heart, O Lord my
    God;
    I will proclaim your greatness for ever.
How great is your constant love for me!
    You have saved me from the grave itself.

Proud men are coming against me, O God;
    a gang of cruel men is trying to kill me –
    people who pay no attention to you.
But you, O Lord, are a merciful and loving
    God,
    always patient, always kind and faithful.
Turn to me and have mercy on me;
    strengthen me and save me,
    because I serve you, just as my mother
    did.
Show me proof of your goodness, Lord;
    those who hate me will be ashamed
    when they see that you have given me
    comfort and help.

CHAPTER 7

THE BIBLE

WHAT'S THE BIG IDEA?

The chapter seeks to show those at all stages of faith that the Bible is relevant to this generation. It also explains something of why it came to have the format it does. Regular Bible reading is encouraged with varying degrees of urgency. For committed Christians there is additional material of some depth about how to apply the Bible to contemporary life by treating it as a book with a particular cultural context and distinguishing the various kinds of writing it contains. They are urged to come under its authority.

PRINCIPAL BIBLE PASSAGE
2 TIMOTHY 3:16-17

OTHER PASSAGES USED
GENESIS 1:1-3; 2:21-22, EXODUS 20:17, DEUTERONOMY 18:9-10; 22:1-2,8, JOSHUA 1:1-2, 1 KINGS 11:3-4, NEHEMIAH 8:1-12, PSALM 98:8; 119:9-18,105, PROVERBS 14:30; 17:12; 22:22-23, ECCLESIASTES 3:1-5, SONG OF SONGS 3:1-4, AMOS 1:6-7, MICAH 6:8-13, MATTHEW 4:1-11; 5:14-16,27-28,41; 13:44; 28:20, MARK 2:13-17, LUKE 1:1-4; 4:14-15; 9:46-48; 10:30-35, JOHN 3:16; 20:30-31, ACTS 17:11, ROMANS 15:4, 1 CORINTHIANS 11:5-10, PHILIPPIANS 4:2-4, COLOSSIANS 2:16-17, 1 THESSALONIANS 4:1-3, 2 TIMOTHY 4:13, 1 PETER 2:17, 2 PETER 1:21, REVELATION 1:12-15; 21:2

MAJOR POINTS THAT CAN BE MADE

◆ The Bible is not a magical book, but one written at specific points in history to tell the story of God's dealings with humankind.

◆ The writers were fallible humans, but they were chosen by God and were 'carried along' by the Holy Spirit as they wrote. As a God-inspired book, Christians can have confidence in its reliability.

◆ By becoming familiar with the ways of Jesus and the rest of the Bible, Christians learn the ways of godly living, which they should apply to their own behaviour.

◆ Attempting to apply the detail of an age-old book does not work; however, coming under the authority of the principles behind the detail is vital for Christians in every generation.

APPROACH 1: INVESTIGATOR

1 GAME (10 minutes)

Pin on to everyone's back a slip of paper bearing the name of an object which was once de rigueur *in order to be in fashion. (The group should not be told that the theme of 'out of date' fashion connects the objects – they should work that out.) They are to discover what object they represent by asking questions of other members of the group. They must be questions with a yes/no answer, and they may not ask the same person two questions* in a row. The objects you choose will vary according to time and place, but here are some suggestions: button-fly jeans, platform sole shoes, cycle pants, boob tubes, flared trousers, flat-top haircuts, wide-lapel jackets, Rubik's cube, white socks, pedal pushers, ra-ra skirts, ankle bracelets, Trivial Pursuit, train-spotting, pop-socks, earmuffs.

At the end of the game ask what the objects had in common. Draw attention to the speed with which clothes, pop groups and leisure activities go out of fashion. Our culture is very different from twenty years ago and hugely different from two thousand years ago. If some people want to argue about the currency of any of the objects, let the discussion continue for a couple of minutes, then move on.

RESOURCES
'AM/PM', SCRIPTURE UNION (DAILY BIBLE READING SCHEME FOR YOUNGER TEENAGERS)
'ALIVE TO GOD', SCRIPTURE UNION (DAILY BIBLE READING SCHEME FOR OLDER TEENAGERS AND ADULTS)
'BIBLE USER'S MANUAL', IVP/SCRIPTURE UNION, 1992
'GOING BY THE BOOK', NIGEL SCOTLAND, SCRIPTURE UNION, 1991
'NEW INTERNATIONAL VERSION', HODDER AND STOUGHTON AUDIO CASSETTE

2 OUT OF DATE? (10 minutes)

Around the wall, put up posters bearing these sentences from the Bible:

1 *In the beginning, when God created the universe, the earth was formless and desolate ... Then God commanded: 'Let there be light' – and light appeared.*

2 *Do not desire another man's house; do not desire his wife, his slaves, his cattle, his donkeys or anything else that he owns.*

3 *Asleep on my bed, night after night, I dreamt of the one I love. I was looking for him, but couldn't find him ... when I found him, I held him and wouldn't let him go.*

4 *Don't take advantage of the poor just because you can ... The Lord will argue their case for them and threaten the life of anyone who threatens theirs.*

5 *The Lord has told us what is good. What he requires of us is this: to do what is just, to show constant love, and to live in humble fellowship with our God.*

6 *You have heard that it was said, 'Do not commit adultery.' But now I (Jesus) tell you, anyone who looks at a woman and wants to possess her is guilty of committing adultery with her in his heart.*

7 *Jesus said, 'I will be with you always, to the end of the age.'*

8 *Respect everyone, love your fellow-believers, fear God and respect the Emperor.*

9 *God loved the world so much that he gave his only Son, so that everyone who believes in him may not die but have eternal life.*

(Genesis 1:1-3, Exodus 20:17, Song of Songs 3:1,4, Proverbs 22:22-23, Micah 6:8, Matthew 5:27-28; 28:20, 1 Peter 2:17, John 3:16)

Beneath each sentence, there should be eight boxes, big enough for everyone present to put ticks in. The members of the group are to read each sentence and may then tick two boxes which seem to apply. Count up and announce the scores. The eight categories are:

- ■ Out of date
- ■ Relevant in a different way from the original meaning
- ■ Waste of time
- ■ Modern-sounding
- ■ Irrelevant
- ■ Significant
- ■ Important once but not now
- ■ Timeless

3 TALK (5 minutes)

Make these points:

☐ *The Bible is not one book, but a collection of 66 books, written over 1000 years. They contain:*
　☐ *The poetic and timeless tale of God beginning his dealings with the world.*
　☐ *The history of his special people, the Jews, a people to whom Jesus belonged.*
　☐ *Books of hymns and wise sayings.*
　☐ *Writings of prophets, passing on messages mainly about how God hates wrongdoing and injustice.*
　☐ *The biography of Jesus.*
　☐ *The story of how the Christian church began.*
　☐ *Letters by leaders of the frst churches about what it means practically to live as Christians.*

☐ *The Bible is not a magic book. It was written centuries ago and thousands of miles from here. That is why it talks about slaves, donkeys and Emperors. It was written by ordinary men and women who could not magically make their words fit the twentieth century in the same way as they fitted the time in which they were written.*

☐ *However Christians believe that the writers were under the control of the Holy Spirit when they wrote (2 Peter 1:21). In that sense it is a book which God has inspired and he meant it to go on teaching people (2 Timothy 3:16-17). Throughout the ages, Christians have chosen not to rewrite it to fit every generation, but to take the principles behind it and apply those to each new century. For example, jealousy is still wrong, even though we are now jealous of our neighbours' sound systems, rather than their donkeys. Because of this, the Bible will never be out of fashion.*

☐ *It isn't a book of mysterious secrets, through which God gives us instant messages. However, by becoming familiar with what*

Jesus did and said, and the way history led up to Jesus and developed from there, Christians learn how they should live. Their experience is that sentences which are centuries old seem personally relevant in a way that no other book can equal (Psalm 119:105).

communicated with or directed him through the Bible in the past. Make this a low-key and frank testimony, so that the Bible comes across as an ordinary, unmysterious part of day-to-day life for God's people.

4 APPLYING THE BIBLE (10 minutes)

Divide the group into subgroups and give each a copy of the sheet 'Part of the Bible' (page 56). Depending on how experienced they are at approaching the Bible, you may need to introduce them to the concept of books, chapters and verses. Then explain a way to apply this kind of biblical material to life – first, working out what it meant to the original hearers; second finding the principles that lie behind it; third applying the principles to today's issues. Show them how the right hand side of the page helps them to do the first two stages, then ask them to read through the passage and talk about the dilemma posed under the heading: 'Now apply it'. After a few minutes, invite them to share their decisions with each other.

5 TESTIMONY (5 minutes)

One of the leaders should explain how he or she uses the Bible in day-to-day life. This could involve explaining how and how often he reads it, whether it is a boring or interesting process and, in particular, how God has

6 DISCUSSION (15 minutes)

Open up the session for discussion. Start by asking the question: 'Are you convinced by those Christians who find the Bible relevant to their lives, or does it still seem out-of-date or remote?' You might also ask: 'What is most likely to stop you reading the Bible, and what might encourage you? What do you find difficult or boring about the Bible?' Encourage teenagers who take the Bible seriously to reply to those who cannot relate to it, rather than the leaders giving more mature answers.

Conclude by showing some of the aids that are available to those who want to find out what the Bible says, including cassettes of the Bible being read in modern translations, which are ideal for personal stereos.

7 PRAYER (5 minutes)

Read Nehemiah 8:1-3,5-6,9-12 (explaining that 'the Law' was part of the Bible available before the time of Jesus). Reflect the pattern of that occasion with a short prayer of praise spoken by the leader (6), a prayer for forgiveness that often we do not take the Bible seriously (9), and a sharing of sweets or drinks as a symbol of the joy God brings (10).

APPROACH 2: *PIONEER*

1 SKETCH (2 minutes)

For five actors (where less actors are available, parts can be doubled up).

Narrator: The Bible, the world's bestseller! Last year the Bible Society alone distributed thirteen million copies. What a useful book! Useful?

A: *(Enters and finds a Bible on the floor.)* A Bible! How useful! It's so stuffy in here, I've been looking for something heavy to prop the door open with. *(She does so and goes.)*

B: *(Finding the Bible in the door.)* A Bible! How useful! *(He opens it up and finds dried flowers in it.)* There aren't many books these days which are suitable for pressing flowers in. *(Puts it on a table on top of the flowers and goes.)*

C: *(Taking the Bible from the table.)* I've found a Bible. How useful! It could bring me good luck. I'll keep it where it can bring me luck every time I pass it. *(She goes to put it on a high shelf. As she does so, it falls and hits her on the head. Staggering back from that, she trips over the table and falls.)*

D: *(Finding the Bible on the floor.)* A Bible! How useful! Oh, it's dirty. A dirty book! Hey hey! Perhaps it's naughty and unexpurgated, full of permissive subjects like sex and blood and violence and seduction. *(He is about to open it, but hesitates.)* No! I'd hate to be disappointed if it wasn't as nasty as I hoped! *(Goes.)*

Narrator: The Bible, the world's most unread bestseller. A survey showed that more than 50% of all those who had a Bible in their home had never opened it. What a useless book! Useless?

A: *(Picks up the Bible, opens it and reads from it, as do the others.)* 'I have studied all these matters to do with Jesus from their beginning, so I thought it would be good to write an orderly account for you. I do this so that you will know the full truth.' Hmm! Interesting!

B: 'In his disciples' presence Jesus performed many other miracles which are not written down in this book. But these have been written in order to prove that Jesus is the Son of God.' Hmm! Intriguing!

C: 'Everything written in the Scriptures was written to teach us in order that we might have hope, through patience and encouragement.' Hmm! Is that so?

D: 'How can a young man keep his life pure? I study your instructions; I examine your teachings. Open my eyes so that I may see the wonderful truths in this book.' Hmm! I wonder!

Narrator: The Bible. Is it worth a second look? There's only one way to find out.

2 TALK (3 minutes)
Make these points:

■◆ **The Bible is not one book, but a collection of 66 books, written over hundreds of years. They contain:**

□ **The poetic and timeless tale of God beginning his dealings with the world.**

□ **The history of his special people, the Jews, a people to whom Jesus belonged.**

□ **Books of hymns and wise sayings.**

□ **Writings of prophets, passing on messages mainly about how God hates wrongdoing and injustice.**

□ **The biography of Jesus.**

□ **The story of how the Christian church began.**

□ **Letters by leaders of the first churches about what it means practically to live as Christians.**

■◆ **Some scholars think the gospels are a more reliable record than any other history book of the same period.**

■◆ **The quotations in the sketch are all adapted from the Bible and show why those who originally wrote it thought it was worth reading.**

■◆ **Christians find that reading the Bible is a more reliable way than any other way to find out what God wants to communicate to them. Sentences which are centuries old suddenly seem personally relevant to them in a way which no other book can equal. Try it and see!**

(Luke 1:3-4, John 20:30-31, Romans 15:4, Psalm 119:9,15,18)

3 WHAT'S STOPPING YOU?
(5 minutes)

Divide the group into subgroups of about three. Give each subgroup a set of six cards, bearing the statements below. Ask: 'What is most likely to stop you reading the Bible?' Between them the subgroups are to decide on a mark out of ten for how likely each is to put them off, and they write it on the card:

✎ I never read books of any kind.
✎ I'm not interested in what it is about.
✎ I'm scared it might make me change.
✎ My friends would think it's naff.
✎ I haven't got a Bible.
✎ It's so irrelevant that it's impossible to understand.

Each subgroup should then be given a further six cards to process in the same way. This time, ask: 'What is most likely to encourage you to read part of the Bible?':

✎ To find out whether Jesus did and said anything worthwhile.
✎ To see if Christians are right.
✎ To find out if it contains mistakes.
✎ I would if some of my friends were trying it.
✎ To see if it can stop me feeling depressed about life.
✎ To discover whether there's any evidence that God exists.

Invite each subgroup to say which statement from each pile came out top. Challenge them in closing not to ignore the Bible. Show them a cassette of one of the gospels in a recent translation and invite them to borrow a part of the Bible to listen to on a *Walkman*, which they can do in private without anyone knowing what they are listening to.

APPROACH 3: *CHALLENGER*

1 MADE FOR SHARING (10 minutes)
Warn the group that you are going to invite them to share with the rest of those present which verse or part of the Bible has been most significant to them in recent months, or simply what their favourite verse is.

One of the leaders or someone known to the group should then give a testimony about how God has communicated with or directed him or her through the Bible, or what he has recently been aware that God is teaching him. He should describe his practice of Bible reading and speak of it as a book which is relevant to his or her own life.

After this prepared testimony, throw open the discussion for the group to talk of significant things they have learnt in the way the leader has described.

2 CONFESSION (5 minutes)
Ask the group silently to consider whether they have been giving the Bible the attention it deserves. After a minute, have a time of confession. The leader should read out Psalm 119:9-16, verse by verse. After each, leave a pause and use this response:

> **Leader:** *Lord, sometimes this is true and sometimes it isn't.*
> **All:** *Forgive us and help us, Lord God.*

Follow this by praying that God will help all present to leave the session able to approach the Bible with more joy and more understanding. Assure them that, as God's forgiven people, there is no need for them to feel guilty any more if they have failed to take the Bible seriously in the past.

3 TALK (5 minutes)
Make these points:

✔ Whenever the Bible talks about Scripture, it is talking about the Old Testament, sometimes just the first five books of it. Jesus knew it well, so well that he could bring it to mind to know what to do when tempted (Matthew 4:1-11). The early Christians studied it fervently to discover whether it still made sense in view of what Jesus had said and done. They found it did. In one church, Berea, they developed the habit of reading it daily (Acts 17:11), a practice that has been copied by Christians the world over.

✔ Paul encouraged a younger man, Timothy, to continue studying the Bible, and commended it to the church in Rome. These are the reasons he gave (2 Timothy 3:16-17, Romans 15:4):
☐ It makes us wise and that helps our faith.
☐ It teaches the truth and shows us when things we hear are in error.
☐ It allows us to correct our faults and live in the right way.
☐ It equips us to do good in our service of God.
☐ It gives us hope by making us patient and encouraging us.

✔ When Jesus returned to Heaven the gospels were not yet written (he himself did not write any books as far as we know). The reasons for this may be that the early Christians were mainly illiterate, there was an ancient tradition of passing on stories by word of mouth, and they thought that Jesus was returning to earth any day so there was no need to write it all down. In fact Jesus' return has taken longer than anyone imagined, so thirty years later it became important to make a record for the new generation since the eye-witnesses were dying out. There were many dodgy stories about Jesus being made up, so the gospel writers made it clear that their plan was to ditch the exaggerated fables and make sure that they gave an absolutely trustworthy report (Luke 1:1-4, John 20:30-31).

✔ The Bible was not dictated into their ears by God as if he were a bird perched on their shoulder. They wrote with their own minds, research, editing, mistakes and different points of view (which means that sometimes differences appear between their records). However, it is clear that these godly men were under the control of the Holy Spirit as they wrote (2 Peter 1:21). This means that we can confidently rely on what they wrote to direct our lives.

4 WHAT KIND OF WRITING? (20 minutes)
Explain that many people ask: 'Is the Bible literally true?' You can't answer that because it is a nonsense question! The Bible contains

many different kinds of writing and to some parts that question does not apply. For instance, 2 Timothy 4:13: 'When you come, bring my coat that I left in Troas' – is that a literal command to today's Christians? It's a nonsense question because 2 Timothy is a letter from one man to another and that is a personal request. The question you should ask starts: 'The Bible is absolutely true. What *kind* of truth is contained in the part I am reading?' And that depends on what sort of writing is in front of you!

Talk about the different kinds of writing, each time asking for someone to read out the examples given. In the New Testament there are:

A Biographical histories (Luke 4:14-15). We are not meant to copy everything done in those days, but we can rely on them to tell what Jesus and the first church were like.

B Parables (Matthew 13:44). Made up stories, but with a challenging truth implicit in them.

C Letters by leaders of the church during the first generation after Jesus advising Christians what to do (Philippians 4:2-4). They are not addressed directly to us, but the principles behind the advice should shape our lives.

D Apocalyptic writings (Revelation 21:2). Deeply creative pictures of how the end of human time will be, like this one of a city wearing a wedding dress, which tells us imaginatively, but not literally, about the splendour and awesomeness of Heaven.

In the Old Testament there are:

E Timeless tales of how God began his plan with humans (Genesis 1:1-3). Here the important question is not, 'Are these scientifically true?' but, 'What is the writer wanting us to learn about God?'

F The Law (Deuteronomy 18:9-10). These were Israel's rules for living. They were written for a nomadic, tent-dwelling community in the desert, so some now seem strange, but there were good reasons for them.

G History of the Jews (Joshua 1:1-2). These stories of Bible 'heroes' are told warts-and-all, so often they give examples to avoid, not copy.

H Songs (Psalm 98:8). Like all lyrics, these words express emotions in metaphors, not straightforward truths.

I Wise sayings (Proverbs 17:12). Practical advice, but not legally binding advice. This verse is not suggesting a trip to the zoo; it is about how dangerous it is to get involved with foolish schemes.

J Prophecy (Amos 1:6-7). Messages from God delivered to Israel and its surrounding nations, usually explaining the anger God feels at wrong-doing and injustice, and what its consequences will be. Here he condemns slavery.

Display a list of references and a list of types of writing (genres). Split the group into subgroups. Ask them to look up the references and decide which reference belongs to which type (rearrange the order in which they are given below). If they finish, ask them to spend the rest of the time discussing what would happen if Christians treated one type as if it were another (eg if the song lyric were obeyed in the way a command of Jesus should be).

Biography	Luke 9:46-48
Parable	Luke 10:30-35
Letter	1 Thessalonians 4:1-3
Apocalyptic	Revelation 1:12-15
Timeless tale	Genesis 2:21-22
Law	Deuteronomy 22:1-2
History of the Jews	1 Kings 11:3-4
Song	Ecclesiastes 3:1-5
Wise saying	Proverbs 14:30
Prophecy	Micah 6:8-13

5 GETTING THE MOST OUT OF IT (20 minutes)

Explain that the Bible is not meant to be used as a book of commands from God personally to us. It doesn't make sense that way. For example, how could we obey the command in 2 Timothy 4:13? So how can we use it, as it teaches us we should, to show us how to live?

Through the years there have been many ways used to apply the Bible, and we need to beware of some of them. Here are four:

1 *Everything in the Bible should be taken at its face value, accepted and obeyed as literally true from generation to generation.*

2 *The New Testament was written for a group of Christians in the first century AD. What it says was important for them. However,* thousands of years have gone past and we now understand far more about God, humans, science and morality. It is what we now know that must shape our lives.

3 There are secrets hidden in the Bible about spiritual warfare and the end of the world. These can only be unlocked by a particular interpretation. (A view particularly likely to produce sects which are sub-Christian.)

4 The Bible was written many years ago for a different culture. We need to work out why God told that culture to act in that way. When we have discovered the timeless principle behind what the Bible says, we must apply it to the new circumstances of our society. We should act in accordance with that principle, not the detail of it.

Most evangelical Christians agree that the fourth approach is the one that best helps us to develop minds and lives like Jesus in our own generation, and all You're Only Young Once! activities are based on it.

Go on to show how the four approaches would treat one particular passage, 1 Corinthians 11:5-10, of which this is an extract:

'Any woman who prays or proclaims God's message in public or worships with nothing on her head disgraces her husband; there is no difference between her and a woman whose head has been shaved. If the woman does not cover her head, she might as well cut her hair. And since it is a shameful thing for a woman to shave her head or cut her hair, she should cover her head ... On account of the angels, then, a woman should have a covering over her head.'

1 The'literal' approach would insist that every woman wears a hat or headscarf when she goes into church.

2 The'then, not now' approach would point out that these words were written for a

completely different age and place. New conditions apply.

3 The 'hidden secrets' approach would make much of the presence of angels in the passage.

4 The 'culture' approach would ask why it was important for women of the time to cover their heads during worship. The answer is that for a woman to uncover her head or have her hair shaved displayed her to be either wantonly defying her husband or a prostitute. It would shock and deeply hurt others who were trying to worship God. That being the principle, how can it be applied today? It is now no longer a sign of being a prostitute to uncover your head or have a hairstyle which involves shaving, so it is acceptable to worship God without a hat. However the verses are not irrelevant, for they do encourage us not to come to church having deliberately dressed to shock or upset people.

Point out that the fourth approach requires a lot more work, but it is the best way to be sure of being godly.

Split the group into subgroups and give them copies of the sheet 'Applying the Bible', which appears on page 57. Invite them to work through it, remembering firstly that they have to decide what kind of writing it is, and secondly that they must find the principle behind its original intention before they can apply it.

After some time working on this, ask the subgroups to comment on anything they found surprising in the exercise, or to mention any features about which they are unsure. In closing, draw attention to the fact that there are many Bible reading aids, particularly daily schemes, which help one go through the process of the 'culture' approach. Encourage everyone to use one regularly.

PART OF THE BIBLE

This is part of the Good News Bible, a translation made from Greek into simple modern English.

Before you can work out how the Bible applies to life today, you need to think about what it meant to its first readers. So there are some facts about life in Jesus' time that you need to know.

Tax collectors were shunned by the Jews because they were working on behalf of the Romans, who had invaded and were occupying the country. Because they could fix their own commission rate, they had a reputation for being rich, crooked and loathed.

Pharisees were paragons of religious respectability, although Jesus often criticised them for hypocrisy.

Jesus had just begun his ministry, and the idea that someone claiming to be a serious religious leader would 'waste' his time in parties with low-life dudes was the first of many deep shocks for strict Jewish leaders.

This shows you which of the 66 books you are looking at.

Each book is divided into several chapters. These are indicated by the large numbers.

Each chapter is divided into many verses. These are indicated by the small numbers.

When put together, it looks like this: Mark 2:6.

This system allows you to find your way around the book. The passage you are going to investigate is Mark 2:13-17.

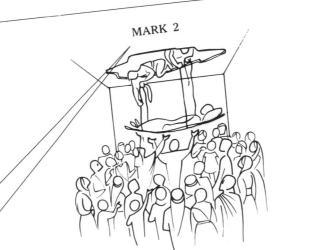

47

MARK 2

Jesus Heals a Paralysed Man
(Matt. 9.1–8; Luke 5.17–26)

2 A few days later Jesus went back to Capernaum, and the news spread that he was at home. ² So many people came together that there was no room left, not even out in front of the door. Jesus was preaching the message to them ³ when four men arrived, carrying a paralysed man to Jesus. ⁴ Because of the crowd, however, they could not get the man to him. So they made a hole in the roof right above the place where Jesus was. When they had made an opening, they let the man down, lying on his mat. ⁵ Seeing how much faith they had, Jesus said to the paralysed man, "My son, your sins are forgiven."

⁶ Some teachers of the Law who were sitting there thought to themselves, ⁷ "How does he dare to talk like this? This is blasphemy! God is the only one who can forgive sins!"

⁸ At once Jesus knew what they were thinking, so he said to them, "Why do you think such things? ⁹ Is it easier to say to this paralysed man, 'Your sins are forgiven', or to say, 'Get up, pick up your mat, and walk'? ¹⁰ I will prove to you, then, that the Son of Man has authority on earth to forgive sins." So he said to the paralysed man, ¹¹ "I tell you, get up, pick up your mat, and go home!"

¹² While they all watched, the man got up, picked up his mat, and hurried away. They were all completely amazed and praised God, saying, "We have never seen anything like this!"

Jesus Calls Levi
(Matt. 9.9–13; Luke 5.27–32)

¹³ Jesus went back again to the shore of Lake Galilee. A crowd came to him, and he started teaching them. ¹⁴ As he walked along, he saw a tax collector, Levi son of Alphaeus, sitting in his office. Jesus said to him, "Follow me." Levi got up and followed him.

¹⁵ Later on Jesus was having a meal in Levi's house.ᵉ A large number of tax collectors and other outcasts was following Jesus, and many of them joined him and his disciples at the table. ¹⁶ Some teachers of the Law, who were Pharisees, saw that Jesus was eating with these outcasts and tax collectors, so they asked his disciples, "Why does he eat with such people?"

¹⁷ Jesus heard them and answered, "People who are well do not need a doctor, but only those who are sick. I have not come to call respectable people, but outcasts."

Now apply it...

In this country, working for the Inland Revenue is a respectable job. But there are other groups whom people find suspect or disreputable, and try to avoid. Who? What would Jesus' attitude to them be? How does that compare with the way they are treated by churches?

APPLYING THE BIBLE

When you build a house, be sure to put a railing round the edge of the roof. Then you will not be responsible if someone falls off and is killed. (*Deuteronomy 22:8*)

Culture: *You need to know that Israelite houses had flat roofs on which people often walked and stored goods.*

Then: *What is the principle behind this?*

_____

Now: *How might this principle be applied today?*

_____

If someone forces you to go one mile, go with him two miles. (*Matthew 5:41, NIV*)

Culture: *You need to know that in Jesus' time, Israel was occupied by an enemy empire, Rome. Roman soldiers were everywhere. They had the right to demand that Jews should carry their packs for them, even if they were heading the opposite way, for a distance of exactly one mile.*

Then: *What is the principle behind this?*

_____

Now: *How might this principle be applied today?*

_____

Let no one make rules about what you eat or drink, or about holy days or the new moon festival or the sabbath. All such things are only a shadow of things in the future; the reality is Christ. (*Colossians 2:16-17*)

Culture: *You need to know that in Colossae, some people were saying that there was a way to be a super-Christian and have more of God's blessing. It involved eating only Jewish food and holding special services to mark every new moon.*

Then: *What is the principle behind this?*

_____

Now: *How might this principle be applied today?*

_____

CHAPTER 8

DOUBT

WHAT'S THE BIG IDEA?

This programme is designed to be reassuring, but also to move teenagers on in their thinking. Doubt is shown to be an acceptable part of Christian experience, but particular areas which are problematic both to believers and non-believers can be talked through in depth. The participants are encouraged to trust God for what they are not sure about on the foundation of what they are sure about. Although suffering is a major area that causes doubt, it is dealt with fully elsewhere, rather than in this chapter.

PRINCIPAL BIBLE PASSAGE
JOHN 20:24–31

MAJOR POINTS THAT CAN BE MADE

◆ Even Jesus' closest friends doubted him at some points. He was not angry, but he did challenge them to belief.

◆ Faith is not the same as proof. It is a positive decision to be certain about what cannot be known, on the basis of evidence and experience of what can be known.

◆ Be honest with Jesus and follow the Bible's advice to stand together as a group, looking at your past, the Christians you admire, and the Bible itself.

OTHER PASSAGES USED
MATTHEW 14:25-33; 28:17,
1 CORINTHIANS 15:3-7, PHILIPPIANS
2:6-11, COLOSSIANS 2:6-7, HEBREWS
11:1-2,39-40; 12:1-2, JAMES 1:6-8,
JUDE 20-25

APPROACH 1: INVESTIGATOR

1 GAME (10 minutes)

Split the group into subgroups in order to play this game. Everyone is to write on a piece of paper four statements about themselves. Three of them should be off-beat, but true, facts which others in the group would probably not already know (for example: 'If I had been born the other gender, my parents were going to call me ...'). The fourth should be a lie.

After time to complete this in secret they should, one at a time, read the four statements to the rest of the subgroup. The others attempt to guess which one is untrue.

RESOURCES
'THE CASE AGAINST CHRIST', JOHN
YOUNG, HODDER AND STOUGHTON
'IT MAKES SENSE', STEPHEN
GAUKROGER, SCRIPTURE UNION

2 BIBLE STORY (5 minutes)

Give everyone a photocopy of the sheet 'Thomas' story' from page 64. Someone should read the story reproduced on that page, which is from John 20:24-31. Display these questions, which the subgroups should briefly discuss:

? How do you think Thomas felt when he saw Jesus and had his doubts removed?

? How would you describe Jesus' attitude to Thomas? Was he, for example, angry?

? Why is it easier for us to believe what we see for ourselves than what people tell us?

3 TALK (5 minutes)
Make these points:

✗ Everyone has doubts. It isn't wrong or sinful! Even the first disciples, face to face with Jesus, had doubts (Matthew 28:17).

✗ Even so, doubts are obstacles for us, and God wants us to have faith. Faith is not the same as proof. It is a conscious decision that we will be certain about things we hope for (Hebrews 11:1).

✗ There is powerful evidence that Jesus was and is God. But that evidence in itself is not proof. We all have experiences which lead us to believe that there is a loving, just, creative God. But those experiences in themselves are not proof. God wants us to trust him when things are too hard to understand or confusing. But that trust in itself is not proof. However, evidence plus experience plus trust equals faith. The three together add up to enough for us to declare our certainty, despite our doubts.

✗ We are told to be merciful to those who doubt (Jude 22). It is right for everyone, whether or not they are Christians, to talk honestly about what they find hard to take. Keep an open mind so that God can operate even in those who are unsure about him. 'How happy are those who believe without seeing me,' said Jesus (John 20:29). He was talking about us.

4 ARE YOU SURE? (10 minutes)
Refer again to the sheet 'Thomas' story', previously distributed. Read out the 24 statements given below. After each one the members of the group, working individually, should decide how they stand in agreement with the statement. If they cannot accept it in any way, they are to write 0 in the box numbered the same as the statement. If they are fully in agreement with it, they write 4 in the box. They may, of course, allocate any number in between (for example, 2 would indicate genuine uncertainty).

1 Advances in science have made chunks of the Bible irrelevant.

2 The only difference between me and an ape is that I have a bigger brain and look prettier.

3 Jesus was a great teacher, but nothing more than that.

4 Praying for someone is a bit like wishing them good luck.

5 The world exists only because of some lucky, cosmic, scientific accident.

6 It doesn't matter what you believe as long as you are sincere about it.

7 All religions are the same, but they approach God in different ways.

8 I am too bad for God to forgive me.

9 Jesus thought he was God, like many crazy people have done since, and persuaded many to believe it too.

10 Jesus was a wonderfully good man, but his followers were wrong to proclaim that he was God.

11 When you pray for something and it happens, that is a coincidence.

12 God is too vast to be interested in me.

13 God obviously doesn't listen to prayers, because usually the thing you ask for does not happen.

14 Emotions, morals and spiritual experiences can all be put down to hormones and chemical reactions.

15 God is angry, not caring.

16 It is relatively easy, when you are in an emotional state, to think that God is responsible for things which are really just ordinary human experiences.

17 The Bible is so full of contradictions that it must have been made up.

18 It's best to leave people be and let them believe what they want to in peace.

19 There is no point in basing your lifestyle on a book which is 2000 years old, like the Bible.

20 Death ends everything for humans.

21 Bible writers invented parts of it so that Jesus' life would not seem like a failure.

22 Jesus thought he was going to change the world, but that all went wrong when he died.

23 There cannot be a loving God when there is so much suffering in the world.

24 It's more important to be good, compassionate and nice than it is to be Christian.

When the chart has been completed, everyone should add up their scores horizontally and put them in the right hand column. They should circle the one with the highest score.

5 DISCUSSION (20 minutes)

The gathering is to reform into up to six groups. They move so that those whose highest total was in row A are in one group, those whose highest total was in row B are in another, and so on. Those with equal highest scores may choose. The leaders should disperse themselves among the groups. If there are six leaders, they should each join one group. If there are three leaders, one should go with groups A and B, one with C and D, one with E and F. If there are two leaders, they should take three groups each, and so on.

The groups that have been formed are arranged in such a way that one subject which often promotes doubt has emerged above the others in each group. The leader attached to the group should have prepared himself or herself in advance to discuss that area of doubt with those for whom it is most problematic. The subjects might loosely be summed up thus:

A The world developed the way it has done by random events; God had no hand in it.

B Jesus was a good man, but not God.

C The Bible is not a reliable guide to history or to lifestyle.

D It does not matter what you believe, as long as you believe it sincerely.

E Answered prayers are coincidences.

F God cannot know and love me individually.

The leaders should start by asking the members of their groups whether they are surprised to find themselves in that group, then invite them to expand on the difficulties they have with this area of the Christian faith. It is important that the leaders are well prepared to listen sympathetically and also to offer positive ways of dealing with each individual doubt. This will require preparatory reading, and the books listed under 'Resources' have precisely the information they will require. This time should not develop into an argument, but new ways of thinking should be offered genuinely in the hope of making progress in one area. It may be wise to go on to talk about an additional subject, about which there was a wider range of scores, so that the groups do not become merely 'matches', with leaders versus teenagers.

6 TRUST GAMES AND PRAYER (10 minutes)

Play some games which illustrate the nature of trust. All of them rely on members of the group trusting each other not to let the others down. There may be doubts as to whether the others are reliable – will they have faith, will doubts diminish their enjoyment or, worst of all, will they be let down? Christians believe that those who put their faith in God could not be let down!

Split into pairs, one standing a pace behind the other. The one in front should shut his eyes, fold his arms, and – without bending – fall backwards in faith that the other one will be ready to catch him.

Those pairs should be brought into a double circle, so that the fallers are in the inner circle facing outwards and the catchers are in the outer circle facing inwards. The pairs should hold each other by the right hand, and cross their left arms over to hold the hand of the person who is standing (from their point of view) to the right of their partner. Once this unbroken criss-cross of arms has been achieved, a person outside the circle should be lifted on to their arms so that he or she is lying between the two concentric rings. By moving their arms up and down, and from left to right, the group should be able to give their passenger a ride all the way round the circle. (Groups of less than twenty should make two parallel lines instead of a circle, and should take great care that the passenger does not fall unexpectedly at the end of the ride.)

Form one larger circle, sitting on the floor with legs stretched out so that feet are tightly packed in the centre. One person should stand upright in the middle, supported by the feet pressing in around her. She should cross her arms across her chest and, keeping completely rigid, without bending her knees, lean toward the edge of the circle. With outstretched arms, the group should take the weight of the person in the centre, and pass her gently round the ring, keeping her feet anchored in the middle.

While the group are still sitting in a circle, invite them to put their arms around each others' shoulders. In that position, the leader should say a prayer thanking God for each other, asking for the trust among the group to develop, and asking that doubts about God will be driven away for those who genuinely want to have faith in him.

APPROACH 2: *PIONEER*

1 *VOTE* (3 minutes)

Put out nine labelled bowls and give each teenager nine matchsticks. They are to vote on whether they believe each of the statements below, which should be written on cards beside the bowls. If they are certain that the statement is true, they put in a whole matchstick. If they have doubts about it, they put the matchstick in broken. (Do not add up the results – it is not a referendum.)

A Someone at Broadcasting House puts records on the Radio One turntable.
B There is a monster in Loch Ness.
C After you go to sleep tonight, you will wake up in the morning.
D There is life on other planets in the universe.
E If we act quickly, we can stop the destruction of the world's resources.
F If you don't drink for a month, you will die.
G You can sail all round the world without dropping off the edge.
H Anne Boleyn, wife of Henry VIII, had six fingers on each hand.
I Walking under a ladder brings bad luck.

2 *TALK* (3 minutes)
Make these points:

◆ *How do we make decisions about what to believe in? Some things we don't have proof of we accept because it is good for us to trust them – for example, at the flick of a switch, invisible airwaves flit miles through space and bring a Radio One DJ's voice from London into your bedroom; it sounds impossibly unlikely, but we take it for granted because it's so enjoyable. Some things we can't prove, but we trust them because life would be intolerable otherwise – for example, we cannot be totally sure of waking up after we go to sleep, but it would be unbearable to stay awake constantly for fear that we might not. Other things we accept because historical evidence, though unprovable, is convincing – Anne Boleyn really did have twelve fingers.*

◆ *What is faith? It is not the same as proof. It is deciding that something is likely enough and good enough to put your trust in as a certainty.*

◆ *In the case of Christianity, the opposite possibilities (that there is no God, the universe is here by a random accident, Jesus was liar, we are all destined for oblivion) are even more doubtful.*

◆ *Jesus accepts people who are not sure. Just be honest with him! If he is there, give him a chance to show himself.*

(Hebrews 1:1-2, Jude 22, John 20:27)

3 *VOTE AGAIN* (3 minutes)

Vote on these 'spiritual' issues in the same way. Make it clear that, once again, this is not a referendum, but a personal statement of belief. God is God whether people believe in him or not.

A The universe was made by God.
B Jesus walked on this planet.
C Jesus was God in human form.
D Jesus rose from the dead.
E If we pray, God hears and responds.
F God loves us individually.
G God is in control of the world.
H Life goes on after death in a spiritual form.
I To be Christian is a good way of life.

4 *CHALLENGE* (1 minute)
'Stop your doubting and believe.' Give it a go. Try praying a bit and see God for what he is! You have nothing to lose but your doubts!

APPROACH 3: *CHALLENGER*

1 *BIBLE STUDY* (10 minutes)

Ask the group to split into subgroups. Display the following references and questions for the subgroups to discuss: Matthew 14:25-33, John 20:24-29, Jude 20-25.

1 Do these passages lead you to believe that doubt makes God angry? Why or why not?

What attitude does Jesus seem to have in each case?

2 What helped Jude's readers to be 'built up in the sacred faith'? What helped Thomas 'stop doubting and believe'? What helped Peter when his doubts began?

3 Which verse would be most likely to encourage you next time doubts are a problem to you, and why?

---

2 TALK (5 minutes)
Make these points:

☐ *Doubt is nothing new. It is no good wishing we could have met Jesus face to face, because even witnesses to his ascension doubted what they saw (Matthew 28:17).*

☐ *God wants us not to doubt, because that makes it easier for him to give us the things he wants for us (James 1:6-8). However, he is merciful when we doubt. As far as he is concerned, even Christians who doubt are faultless because of what Christ has done to forgive us. He is able to uphold us (Jude 22, 24).*

☐ *Doubting can be part of the way in which we make progress with God, for he can bring us through to a stronger faith. A few suggestions for helping yourself through it:*
☐ *Go back in mind to the time you first believed and remind yourself what convinced you when you accepted Jesus (Colossians 2:6-7).*
☐ *Think of the example of great Christians from the past and present (Hebrews 11:1-2, 39-40; 12:1-2). Pray with others and stick together in appreciating that God loves you (Jude 20-21). Keep your faith strong by reading the Bible; that's why John wrote his gospel (John 20:30-31).*

☐ *As we struggle through doubt, we can emerge like Peter, saying to Jesus: 'Truly you are the Son of God' (Matthew 14:33).*

---

3 DISCUSSION (35 minutes)
Suggest five things that are often problematic for non-believers, and for Christians too. They are doubts which nag at people. Mention them one at a time, giving the subgroups a chance to discuss each one and

decide: 'How would I respond to someone who told me in conversation that their faith was held back by this doubt?'

1 God does not really exist; we're all here by a random scientific accident, followed by its logical consequences.

2 Jesus was a great human, but the miracles, and especially the resurrection, are too irrational to believe. He was not God.

3 Answered prayers are coincidences, or may be God acting randomly.

4 Death ends everything; there is no way of being sure of anything afterwards.

5 God can't love me personally; I'm too much of an awful, guilty, wicked person.

Each time, after discussion, the subgroups report themselves to be in one of three positions:

A This doubt is a genuine problem for us.
B We accept that this is untrue, but we don't know how we would talk to someone who argued for it strongly.
C We accept that this is untrue, and we could discuss it with confidence.

Having spent this short time on each of the five, the leader should decide which one or two of the doubts could usefully be discussed further. Open that one up for a longer discussion, asking those for whom it is not a problem to help the others understand how they have worked through it.

---

4 CREED (10 minutes)
Explain that a creed is a statement about belief in God, in Jesus, in the Holy Spirit. It is designed to be spoken aloud by a group of Christians so that they can go public on what they believe. Some date back to within a very few years of Jesus' return to heaven, but most were written during the first four centuries AD.

Read some of them, including the very early:

> **Christ has died,**
> **Christ is risen,**
> **Christ will come again.**

Some of them are quoted by Paul in the Bible, which means they must have been in wide circulation before about 60 AD. Read Philippians 2:6-11 and 1 Corinthians 15:3-7.

Then introduce the one used most widely today, the Apostles' Creed, from about 400 AD:

We believe in God, the Father almighty,
creator of heaven and earth.
We believe in Jesus Christ, his only Son,
* our Lord.*
He was conceived by the power of the
* Holy Spirit,*
and born of the Virgin Mary.
He suffered under Pontius Pilate,
was crucified, died, and was buried.
He descended to the dead.
On the third day he rose again.
He ascended into heaven,
and is seated at the right hand of the
* Father.*
He will come again to judge the living and
* the dead.*
We believe in the Holy Spirit,
the holy catholic Church,
the communion of saints,
the forgiveness of sins,
the resurrection of the body,
and the life everlasting. Amen.

Ask the subgroups to work together to write a creed to express the facts about God, about Jesus and about the Holy Spirit that they most want to affirm. Give them several minutes to work on this until they are agreed on some phrases which they can collectively agree beyond doubt. If there are statements about which the subgroup are not all certain, but which are biblical, encourage them to include the statements as an acknowledgement that the words are from God and are honourable. Invite each subgroup to stand and say their creed together as an affirmation of, and encouragement to, faith.

THOMAS' STORY

One of the twelve disciples, Thomas (called the Twin), was not with them when Jesus came. So the other disciples told him, 'We have seen the Lord!'

Thomas said to them, 'Unless I see the scars of the nails in his hands and put my finger on those scars and my hand in his side, I will not believe.'

A week later the disciples were together again indoors, and Thomas was with them. The doors were locked, but Jesus came and stood among them and said, 'Peace be with you.' Then he said to Thomas, 'Put your finger here, and look at my hands; then stretch out your hand and put it in my side. Stop your doubting and believe!'

Thomas answered him, 'My Lord and my God!'

Jesus said to him, 'Do you believe because you have seen me? How happy are those who believe without seeing me!'

In his disciples' presence Jesus performed many other miracles which are not written down in this book. But these have been written in order that you may believe that Jesus is the Messiah, the Son of God, and that through your faith in him you may have life.

A	2	20	14	5	=
B	9	3	22	10	=
C	19	17	1	21	=
D	6	18	24	7	=
E	13	4	11	16	=
F	12	23	8	15	=